THINK

Like a
BLACK BELT

Jim Bouchard

Printed in the United States of America
San Chi Publishing
sanchionline.com

First Printing: May 2010

ISBN-13 978-0-578-05750-7

Trying to dedicate a book is always a trying process! There are too many people involved to thank everyone by name without leaving some important people out, I'll do my best.

First, thanks to all the students, parents and instructors at Northern Chi Martial Arts Center. Your continued support and encouragement allows me to reach out and share the message of Black Belt Mindset with others. Thanks particularly to the members of our Black Belt community; this is your story.

Special thanks to Dan Bosse, Paul Clark, Rich Wells, Mike Mason, Rol Fessenden and Tony Lacroix for holding down the fort.

Thanks to some new friends including Dr. John Tantillo for your amazing support, advice, encouragement and generosity. Thanks to Jon Hansen, George Krueger, Mary-Lynn Foster and Dr. Jackie Black who always see more in my work than I do; you're all easily amused and I appreciate it! Thanks to Larry Winget, your kind endorsement and wonderful advice came at just the right time and as always thanks to William R. Patterson whose wisdom and generosity is always greatly treasured!

Thanks also to Dennis McClellan at DC Press, Neil Ducoff, Gerald Walsh, Mark Altman, Larry Adams, Joan Sotkin, Marsha Petrie Sue, Sally Shields, Ken Lizotte and all my other new friends and mentors whose kind words, thoughtful critique and encouragement is so valuable to me. Thanks to Ashley Lawson for her patience and sense of humor that made the editing process simple and easy and to Joe & Michelle Carpine and Ben Sawyer who perfectly captured the spirit of this project and delivered the Black Belt look!

Thanks to my dear friends and mentors Don Lonsway, David Melville, Steve Wallace, Peter Storey, Geoff Lamdin, Bob LaBrie, David Lee, Henry Guidiboni, and "Old Sensei" Poppa Bill Sergiy, Jim Ambrose, Peter Jordan, Grandmaster Mark Shuey, Dr. Yang, Jwing-Ming, Dave Marquis and all the wonderful martial artists who are part of my life as teachers, friends and training partners. Special mention to Master Chris Keith who is not only a part of my martial arts life, but whose generous contribution polished this stone into a mirror.

As always thanks to Alexandra Armstrong. You're always in the ring with me.

For this one, special thanks to Smokey Hicks was always ringside throughout this project. Every time I was knocked down, it was Smokey who said "get up!"

There are too many heroes, teachers, friends & supporters in my life to thank everyone personally. I sincerely hope you all know how important you are to this work and to me, and I'm grateful every day for every one of you.

"When you hear the words Black Belt, you immediately think of other words like 'as good as it gets' and 'the best.' What does it take to actually be the best? It takes a mindset - a way of thinking. Jim, a real black belt himself, does a great job teaching you to be your best by obtaining the mindset that will propel you to excellence. Read this book!"

Larry Winget
Television personality and 5 time *New York Times/Wall Street Journal* bestselling author of *Your Kids Are Your Own Fault* and *The Idiot Factor*
LarryWinget.com

"...I've had thousands of experts on my show - Jim Bouchard stands out among the best. For top shelf advice, Think like a Black Belt offers easy-to-understand tips and it's packed with invaluable ideas. Read this book, it will improve your bottom line personally and professionally."

Kurt Schemers
Creator and host of Traders Nation™
KurtSchemers.com

"Jim has hit the nail on the head by focusing on perfection, confidence and leadership. This is a must read for anyone looking for the next level of success and increasing the enjoyment of life. Just wonderful!"

Marsha Petrie Sue
Author of *The Reactor Factor* and *Toxic People*
MarshaPetrieSue.com

"Think Like a Black Belt silences the inner voice of self-doubt and provides you with the confidence, wisdom and tools to know that you can handle yourself in any situation. From corporate executive to professional athlete, if you've ever wanted to do more or to become more, this is the book that will help you realize your greatness."

William R. Patterson
Best-selling Co-author of *The Baron Son*
BaronSeries.com

"*Think Like a Black Belt has got to be one of the funniest, most motivating, clever and engaging books I've read in a long time! Jim's philosophy and teachings are very, very powerful! He is honest, witty, to the point, and uses examples from everyday life that will make you laugh and cry! Filled with wisdom and practical advice, Think Like a Black Belt contains the components of how to be successful in every area of your life, and to change the things that have been holding you back. I loved every page of this book and couldn't put it down. Jim Bouchard has truly created an awe-inspiring gem for anyone in the pursuit of excellence. Filled with both spiritual nuggets and simple to understand and implement, I am confident that you will love this book!*"

Sally Shields
Speaker, radio personality, publicity specialist and
author of the #1 Amazon.com bestseller, *The Daughter-in-Law Rules!*
theDILRules.com

"*Whether you're in a state of bliss, recovery from anything, or despair, Think Like a Black Belt fits your times. In Outliers, Malcolm Gladwell makes the point that talent is the will to practice. Jim Bouchard's wisdom sharpens this point and helps write its wisdom on every aspect of human life. Frustrated perfectionists will draw immense relief from his pages. Those who've given up on a passion -- or anything -- will as well. Think Like a Black Belt will cause you to act with courage, humility, and character you -- and, likely, many around you -- doubt you possess. This work sets off a viral strength, written with a candor that rings with joy. Oscar Wilde said "it's good to be expected, yet not to arrive." Though it's never good when we fail to arrive on shores of the true greatness of which we are capable -- as individuals and larger communities. Test me on this: After reading Think Like a Black Belt, you will expect more of yourself. You will rise above the low expectations too commonly thrown against us, especially in hard times. It's as though Jim Bouchard picked up and ran with the great theme of William Faulkner, who in his Nobel acceptance speech predicted that humankind will not merely survive, but will prevail. Thank you Jim for helping show the world the way to prevail, no matter the challenges before us. Bravo on Think Like a Black Belt.*"

"*I completely recommend this book, especially to recovering addicts and their spouses and children, anyone who's ever known the heartbreaks of destructive relationships, and all who desire to unleash the benevolent, world-changing force of our inner power!!*"

Michael Cogdill
24-time Emmy winner/holder of the National Edward R. Murrow for Feature Reporting in television
Author of *She-Rain*, a novel of extravagant love triangle in the American South
Author of *Cracker the Crab and the Sideways Afternoon*, a children's book designed to raise self-esteem in the young.
http://she-rain.blogspot.com/

TABLE OF CONTENTS

INTRODUCTION

I began writing this book in the midst of America's worst economic recession since the Great Depression. People are losing jobs, businesses, and homes. Too many people have lost their savings and retirement as our banking and investment system implodes. Others are taking jobs well beneath their training, talents and abilities just to get by. Too many others are selling their homes at a loss or returning to work after earning a well-deserved retirement.

The recession has affected the entire world. Our world is now completely connected and inter-dependent. The global economy is no longer a dream or specter depending on your perspective; it is a reality that we all should try to understand and that we all have to live with. Conditions and circumstances well beyond your control can dramatically affect and impact your life no matter where you live or work.

Some pundits predict the imminent collapse of the "American way." Others are saying our position as a world power has wavered and we are beginning a period of inevitable decline. Our day in the sun is over.

I say BULLSHIT!

I remain confident; I think like a Black Belt. I think like a Black Belt because I am a Black Belt. Much of what I'm going to share with you comes from my life as a professional martial artist.

Whether you're a CEO, a janitor, a mom or dad, or anyone reading this book…

You too, can think like a Black Belt!

I have been a martial artist for nearly 25 years. In that time, I've been blessed with incredible teachers, wonderful students, and amazing adventures. Most importantly, I've learned how to apply the process of martial arts mastery to my personal and professional life.

In 2006, I decided I'd like to try and share this process with people. I thought to myself, "Why can't people who aren't martial artists apply the same principles to make themselves feel powerful and create success in whatever they'd like to achieve?" That's when I wrote my first book, ***Dynamic Components of Personal POWER***.

One of the fundamental truths about practicing martial arts is this:

"Perfection is not a destination, it's a never-ending process!"

When I finished ***Dynamic Components of Personal POWER*** I thought I had my life's mission pretty well mapped out. Of course, thinking like a Black Belt I also knew as soon as I finished my book that I was going to start the process of refining those thoughts and improving how I would teach those components to the public. My intention was to instruct people on developing and applying power for personal and professional success.

To a martial artist, a "kata" is never finished. A kata is a set of movements used to teach, learn, and practice martial arts movements. A kata is never perfect. If you're sincere as a martial artist, a kata is always in a constant process of perfection. This isn't a carrot and stick thing; it's simply an acknowledgement of the wonderful human condition. Nikos Kazantzakis said it better than I can in ***Zorba the Greek***. In this amazing story, the main character, Zorba, grabs life one fistful at a time. He teaches us that one's journey is about embracing the "full catastrophe" of life. It's about appreciating the gift of life by living to our fullest capacity in every moment. It's accepting that the meaning of life is to create a meaning for your own life; and that's accomplished by living it, not by accomplishing any particular goal or status and proclaiming yourself finished.

Mastering a martial art, or a business art or any other worthwhile skill is not a matter of attaining any particular title, level, or recognition. It's about learning and accepting this process of perfection and dedicating the rest of your life to it. It's about living in a constant state of self-perfection where happiness doesn't depend on satisfaction, but on the joy of the adventure. It's about accepting challenge, pain, adversity, and hardship as partners. It's about developing courage to face your own weaknesses and deciding to do something about it. Most of all, mastery is about taking personal responsibility for your success and happiness, while doing what it takes to get there, especially when times are tough.

There are always going to be tough times. They may be due to decisions you've made and circumstances you've brought on yourself or due to circumstances and conditions beyond your control. No matter who you are and no matter what circumstances and conditions you're now facing, you can create your own vision of personal and professional success and happiness; and you can achieve it. I know because I did it. More importantly, I know this because I am still doing it.

I know this as truth: If I learned to think like a Black Belt you can too.

How, exactly, do you *"Think Like a Black Belt?"*

What we're going to do in the next several chapters is break down the most important characteristics of what I call "Black Belt Mindset." I could have picked dozens of characteristics to talk about, but when one thinks like a Black Belt one looks for simplicity.

So, let's keep it simple!

Most of this book will focus on three major areas of Black Belt Mindset. Focus on these areas of personal development and you'll go a long way toward becoming a Black Belt Mindset Master in your personal and professional life.

1. Perfection: The first step in thinking like a Black Belt is to dedicate yourself to constant self-perfection and personal development. A Black Belt Master never stops improving, learning and evolving. In this section I'll discuss how Excellence, Discipline and Focus will help you embrace a process of continual self-perfection.

2. Confidence: When I ask people for the most obvious traits of someone who has earned a Black Belt the answer is usually "confidence." Confidence is at once an inner sense of surety and at the same time an outward projection of one's faith in one's own ability to perform. Here we'll explore Power, Perseverance and Mastery and how each of these characteristics builds the self-confidence and faith you need to seek and face the challenges that lead you to your adventures.

3. Leadership: Human beings are interconnected beings. The ultimate expression of sharing is leadership; not in the sense of dominance or control, but in the sense of expanding one's presence in the world through teaching and living as an example for others. I'll talk about how to develop the essential characteristics of effective leadership: Courage, Compassion and Wisdom.

These are some of the characteristics we'll be looking at. No matter what you do, you can adopt and apply these same characteristics in your life. My intention is to introduce what I've found to be the most fundamental and important characteristics that are most applicable to real life, even if you never want to throw a kick or punch!

I'm sure you'll recognize some of these characteristics in your own life. At the very least, you'll recognize their importance. You might feel you need some work in one or more of these areas; that in itself is an expression of Black Belt Mindset. A Master is never really satisfied, but looks at himself as a constant work in progress.

The characteristics we'll talk about in this short book are those I've found to be the most universal. In my experience in life and martial arts I've learned that there is tremendous power in working with, rather than against natural forces. It's our nature to be powerful and productive; we all look for some meaning and importance to our lives.

On the mat, a Black Belt knows that working with natural forces and the force of an enemy is much more effective than working against these forces. Real life works the same way! Develop more awareness about your natural talents, abilities and passions, and you greatly improve your chances of living a productive, creative, happy, and successful life.

One of the most important and fundamental reasons for living is self-perfection. It's our nature to want to learn, grow and improve. It's also our nature to want to share ourselves with others. People engaged in these processes tend to be the most happy, successful and productive.

Simple, not easy! In fact, earning a Black Belt is simple; the keys are dedicated practice and perseverance. Keep practicing and you'll get to Black Belt! It's not always easy. It's sometimes painful, frustrating, boring, and tedious. On the way, you'll doubt yourself and you'll subject yourself to the sometimes harsh criticism of your teachers.

Isn't it the same way in real life? As you learn to think like a Black Belt, you may feel a bit overwhelmed at times. If this happens, return to the basics. When a Black Belt is struggling with a technique, we break it down to the most basic movements, even a simple punch or kick, and work from there. When it's not easy, come back to simplicity!

Excellence is your nature. Mankind is an explorer, builder and conqueror. You don't have to conquer others to honor this human nature; you have to conquer your "self." After all, every Black Belt knows that your most formidable opponent is not external; your most formidable opponent is you!

Let's bow in and get to work!

HOW DOES A BLACK BELT THINK?

Something happens when you tie on your Black Belt for the first time, at least it happened for me and for the students I've promoted to the most recognizable rank in martial arts. There's a great feeling of pride and accomplishment; that probably seems obvious. When the rank is earned properly, there's also an almost overwhelming feeling of humility, maybe even unworthiness.

A Black Belt test is an incredible experience. In most systems, this test will challenge every aspect of a martial artist's skill, knowledge, and endurance; but most of all, it challenges the will to continue. The strange thing is that when someone genuinely earns a Black Belt, that person wonders why, given all the mistakes and flaws still left to polish out, he or she is being honored with the ultimate symbol of skill and achievement.

Everyone brings an individual agenda to the Black Belt experience. I've promoted several military personnel and veterans, people who have served in real battle, and more than one has told me that their Black Belt test was one of the most challenging experiences of their lives. Why?

It certainly was for me; but I'm a guy who spent most of my young adult life with no sense of self-worth or self-esteem. I had never, at least in my mind, actually completed any worthwhile endeavor. I'm a two-time college drop-out who spent most of the early 1980's lost in the fog of the legendary trilogy of sex, drugs, and rock and roll. Well, I could have done a little better in the sex department, but I more than made up for it with the others.

When I earned my Black Belt it marked a transition point in my life. From that moment forward I wouldn't be the drop out or the former junkie; I'd be a Black Belt. I wouldn't be the guy who never finished anything; I'd be a Black Belt. Working hard for a meaningful accomplishment can change your life. In martial arts we call this "Kung Fu" and I've got to tell you it works!

Oh, I still had plenty of work to do. After 25 years in martial arts I still have plenty of work to do. "Perfection isn't a destination; it's a never ending process." Still, I knew for the first time in my life that I could transform my "self" and accomplish anything within the scope of my talents and abilities. I knew for the first time in my life that I was somebody of value.

In 1994 I started my first martial arts center. Within a couple of years I split from my original association and founded Northern Chi. Since that time I've promoted over 100 people to Black Belt and counting. I've seen lawyers, doctors, teachers, business owners, professors, psychiatrists, therapists, police officers, firefighters, CEOs, and at least one federal judge all earn their Black Belts, and of course those military folks, some high-ranking officers I mentioned earlier.

To this day I still wonder why the hell any of these people come to me for instruction. I know I have a skill that these people want to learn, but what could people so accomplished, so educated, so evolved in their own professions learn from a college drop-out who was barely squeezing a living out of a small town karate school? Why would these people want to study with me? Why did these talented, skilled and educated people want to learn how to beat people up?

Every person has a story, and every person I admire never finishes their story. Each martial artist comes to the Black Belt experience with a unique agenda. That's why it's such a remarkable individual challenge no matter what one has done before.

You'll find the military officer who is more comfortable leading troops into battle than guiding his own son through the misery of asking for his first date. You'll find the judge who appreciates that the rank he's earning is one of the few authentic moments of recognition in a career where doing his job well often means being part of the destruction of other people's lives. You'll find the doctor who spends her life healing others, but has never learned to heal herself and the psychologist who finds it easier to know your mind than his own. You'll find the CEO who understands that to earn the respect of his employees he is someone who is constantly learning new skills in the office and out.

You'll also find the adult who at last is facing a fight he ran away from in the 7th grade. The ex-wife who is, for the first time, finding the courage to stand up to the abusive ex-husband she'll never actually see again face to face, or the woman who is finally learning how to deal with the rapist she barely escaped years ago.

You'll meet the guy whose doctor told him he better get in shape or face a life of chronic heart problems, and the woman who always wanted to learn martial arts and found the motivation after watching her kids do it.

…And to be honest, you'll meet a lot of people who really bought into the mystique of the Black Belt. A lot of these folks grew up watching Bruce Lee and Toshiro Mifune. We saw "Billy Jack" and "Black Belt Jones." Without even realizing it, the martial arts slowly became part of our culture through James Bond, The Green Hornet and Chuck Norris. The new generation followed Jackie Chan and now Lucy Liu and Ben Watanabe. They've grown up in a martial arts world with Power Rangers, Karate Kids, and Crouching Tigers.

Most of the current generation only knows David Carradine from "Kill Bill." Many of us who have been around awhile came to the arts because we wanted to be the wise, mysterious and very cool Kwai Chang Caine from the "Kung Fu" TV show.

No matter how you start, every single person who earns a Black Belt is transformed by the experience through your own unique set of challenges. You face your own demons, overcome your own weaknesses, and cultivate your own strengths. Earning a Black Belt is, above all, an incredibly enlightening individual experience…if you do it right!

The right way to do it is with humility. Not the sanctimonious, self-righteous, self-serving type of fake humility too common in our culture, but the authentic humility that comes from the appreciation that one's achievement is the product of hard work, painful introspection, and a commitment to continual self-improvement. This humility celebrates your own part in the process of achievement and honors the part your teachers, advisors, and supporters have in your success.

You earn your Black Belt and the honor is yours alone; at the same time you cannot do it by yourself.

STOP! This isn't a book about martial arts or martial artists; it's a book about how you can think like one whether or not you actually want to punch or kick to earn a Black Belt.

The background information is important; however, at some point I began to understand why all these people came to me and what it was they were really trying to learn.

Some years ago I attended a seminar to learn how to improve enrollment in my martial arts centers. As I remember it, the presenter was not a Black Belt or even a martial artist; he was a master salesman. He asked what should have been a pretty simple question: "When people come into your academy, what do they want?"

The answer seemed pretty simple too; most of us agreed that anyone walking in to a martial arts school wanted to learn martial arts. Variations on the theme included a desire to learn self-defense, build self-confidence, fitness…blah, blah, blah. We all sounded exactly like the boiler plate yellow page ads each of us ran in our local newspapers.

The presenter let us punch ourselves out, slipped neatly and knocked us out with a single counter-punch. "No" he said, "They want to be YOU!"

We spend our lives as Black Belts trying to find simplicity in the midst of complexity. The presenter was exactly right. Sure, people might be looking for all the benefits we place in bullet points on our brochures; but most of all, they want to be Black Belts. They usually don't say that, in fact most people on their first visit will say they're not even thinking about making it all the way to Black Belt. They've heard about how hard it is, how long it takes and they know about the pain, frustration and misery that goes along with it. Still, somewhere there is this simple motivating thought: "Wouldn't it be cool to be a Black Belt?"

This salesman brought it all into focus. My students simply want to be like me; at least as far as they see me in my role as Black Belt Master. I can admit today that when I started, I often imagined myself standing proudly, like my Master, with the Black Belt strapped across my waist. More than that, I wanted to have the poise, confidence, and wisdom I saw in the Black Belt Masters I was blessed to train with.

Isn't that at least part of the reason you're reading this book? With sincere humility, I'm not stroking my own ego imaging an affirmative answer to that question. If you were attracted by the title, cover, or theme of this book you've probably reached a point in your life where you either:

• Want to make a significant change in your life.

• Or…recognize that continual change is the only meaningful constant.

Either way, it's time to Think Like a Black Belt! I'm humbled and honored to be your guide.

I'm going to assume that there's a decent chance you're not really interested in learning how to punch, kick, or defend yourself. You may be solely interested in learning Black Belt Mindset so you can become more effective in your personal or professional life. That's OK; but I will say that you might consider enrolling in a martial arts program at some point. Today there's a system and art for everyone, any age, any condition, and any personality.

Our craft ranges from the gentle practice of Tai Chi to the devastating power and aggressiveness of modern Mixed Martial Arts. In between there are hundreds of different styles, forms and practices. Each puts particular emphasis on some aspect of the arts from the philosophy of mind/body connection to the practical self-defense applications, and to the highest levels of competitive arts. It's a great activity for kids, whether the kid is 3 or 103, and it's a wonderful experience for the entire family. The "fighting families" are some of the most wonderfully close and connected families I've ever met.

Now that I've fulfilled that obligation let's move along!

Whether or not you want to actually become a martial artist is not important. The principles and characteristics of Black Belt Mindset work at home, in school, the office, business, or when facing life's most challenging moments. You don't need to be a Black Belt to think like one; or to put it another way, you can be a Black Belt in any profession or vocation from CEO to Mom. You can adopt a mindset of excellence, discipline, and self-confidence in any area of your life…

…you will, however, have to commit to the training!

That's what this book is about. I earned my first Black Belt in 1991. I've trained well over a hundred people who have become Black Belts in Kenpo Karate. I've trained thousands of people to think like Black Belts in personal and professional life.

Throughout this book I'll teach you how to cultivate and apply Black Belt Mindset. This is a mindset of action and power. I ask that you use this mindset to first improve yourself, then to improve the lives of people around you by preparing them to accept responsibility and recognize opportunity.

This isn't a "power of positive thinking" manual. There are plenty of those; some are great, and others frankly suck. The fact is that thought is not enough; results are a product of thought converted to action. If you want to accomplish something, you've got to get off your ass and actually do something!

Positive thought is an essential ingredient in positive action. You don't need to be a Master or a genius to know that. How much do you accomplish when you're in a negative mindset? Positive thought opens your mind to possibility. Open yourself to the endless possibilities around you and you greatly increase your probability of success.

For the record, the positive thinking books and teachers that suck are those who promise you that through positive thought all your dreams will come true. It's irresponsible to leave the blood, sweat and tears out of the adventure. These people are teaching a quick fix, an easy road to success and happiness. There isn't one, and even if there was I wouldn't tell you about it.

The real magic lies in learning how to enjoy the journey with all the twists and turns. Sometimes you're rolling along with open road and clear skies; at other times you're slogging along hip deep in mud. You may as well enjoy every step, or at least learn how to endure the muddy parts without losing your mind!

The first step is to accept full personal responsibility for your own adventure. As soon as you tie on your first white belt and step on the mat, you realize that only one person is going to transform you into a Black Belt. Sneak a peak in the mirror and you're looking at him!

When we promote a student to Black Belt at Northern Chi we make it an elegant experience. I'm seated in the traditional Japanese kneeling position of "seiza" below a square wooden platform. Our other current Black Belts and instructors are seated with me. The candidate kneels on the platform, above us, to accept the rank.

During the ceremony we acknowledge the contribution of instructors, family members, fellow students, and friends who all play a supporting role in the achievement of the rank. However, when the candidate steps up to this platform, we're recognizing the incredible individual effort required to earn the Black Belt. You can only earn the rank by accepting full responsibility for your training, your mindset, and your performance.

As you learn to think like a Black Belt, it's essential to accept this responsibility. You'll utilize the teaching, advice and encouragement of others who support you in your adventure; and it's your obligation to be grateful for it. These folks include teachers, mentors, advisors, and also the friends and family who offer their understanding and support for what you're doing. Ultimately, your success is solely your own responsibility. You're the nexus of all these people and resources, and you're the embodiment of their contribution to your success.

Self-improvement is sometimes lonely business. It may even seem selfish at times, but the least selfish thing you can do for others is to improve your "self." If you really want to help others, make yourself better. That's how you become a better resource to your family, your business, your community, and the world. If everyone is simply focused on being the best they can be, it all works out!

This adventure is about becoming a "Master." Your journey to personal mastery begins with a simple decision. Decide to commit yourself to continual self-perfection, and don't expect anyone to do this work for you.

These days too many people expect others to make life better for them. It is nobody else's job to make your life better; but it is your job to express your gratitude if they do. If someone gives you a job, be grateful. If someone gives you an opportunity, a place to live, a scholarship, or help with feeding your children; be grateful. If someone kicks you in the ass once in a while, be grateful!

If you want more, take responsibility for your own happiness and go get it for yourself.

Be Your Own Teacher

There comes a time in every martial artist's life when they have to leave the Master. It's not usually that the Master doesn't have more to offer, it's simply a fact that experience is your best teacher and you have to go out and earn that on your own.

Even when you're still under someone's tutelage you are still responsible for your own learning. Whether you're a student or a parent of a student, you need to burn this wisdom into your head:

"The teacher's job is simply to teach; it's the student's job to learn."

That's a wonderful old fortune cookie saying as true today as it was long ago. Here are some rather shocking clichés you'll hear today:

"My teacher sucks!"

"This school is really not doing enough for my child."

"My child is really not challenged enough in school."

In some cases, any of these statements might be valid; so what? A teacher's responsibility is to share knowledge and deliver a curriculum. It's certainly a blessing when you've got a teacher who is caring, creative and responsive to the individual needs of students. I also happen to think that if you accept the responsibility of teaching, it is your obligation to be caring, creative and responsive. Still, you can be the best teacher in the world and still be stuck with students who are lazy, disrespectful, and unmotivated.

I tell my students that I'm "Sensei," not "Slappy the Clown." It's not a teacher's job to entertain or to force learning on a student, at any age. It's the student's job to learn and to do one's best with the information and knowledge the teacher is sharing. If a teacher happens to be engaging and entertaining as well, that's an added blessing; be grateful.

The same thing goes for training on the job. It's not your employer's obligation to make you a better person or even a better employee. An enlightened employer will see the value in providing job training and the opportunity for advancement and personal development; if you're employed by such a company, be grateful.

It's your job to make yourself better so you can improve your prospects for success and happiness. If you want to get ahead and your employer isn't helping you, go out and get the training you need on your own. Your employer's obligation ends with your paycheck.

To be your own teacher, you must accept full responsibility for your own development. It's your trip, start making tracks.

A Black Belt knows that the Master can share knowledge, wisdom and experience. The Master provides criticism and correction, while the student does the work. Your own experience will be your most important teacher.

In school and at the workplace too many people wait around for some secret or savior. Don't wait. Accept responsibility for your own development and embrace a lifelong pursuit of learning and self-perfection.

Parents: Send your kids to school prepared to learn. Later, send them to the job prepared to work. If I'm talking to my junior students, I tell them it's their job to pay attention in school, ask for extra assignments if they're bored and be respectful even if they don't like their teachers. If I'm talking to their parents, I tell them it's their job to teach their children how to pay attention in school, model respectful behavior and insist on it from their children, and if they feel their child is not being challenged it's their obligation to find new ways to expand their minds through reading and other adventures.

I've had the honor to work with many incredible parents and families. The happiest families are always those who accept full responsibility for their children's learning experience. These parents are grateful for the efforts of teachers but never expect the school to provide all of their children's education. They don't expect me to "make" their kids practice their kenpo and they support me when I tell kids it's their job to practice, not mine and not their parent's.

Simple, Not Easy

A Black Belt is always looking for simplicity. When you watch a martial artist perform an intricate set of movements it might look as if we really enjoy complexity; not so! Any complex set of movements is really a series of simple ones. Mastery is the ability to combine these simple movements into a flowing, dynamic sequence with grace, speed and power.

You can reduce any complex set of techniques to simple, basic movements. You can also reduce any complex issue in life or business to basic, component parts that are always more understandable and manageable.

The key to mastery is simply practice. Practice is also the only authentic "secret" to the martial arts and life. The paradox of "simple, not easy" is that while almost anything can be reduced to simple elements, it requires a great deal of practice and hard work to make it look and feel easy!

Once a Black Belt breaks a movement down to its most basic components, he goes to work polishing and perfecting that movement until it is instinctive, flowing and powerful. When you're working on a quantum level in martial arts, improvement is going to be subtle and progress is a slow process that takes time.

I tell my students that by the time they reach Black Belt, they probably understand how to express about 90% of their power in any basic movement. We spend the rest of our lives looking for the last 10%!

That last 10% comes in very small, subtle increments. You're working with very basic movement and seemingly endless repetition to gain even the smallest increase in power. Basic movements are naked; there's no place to hide flaws. That's why the simplest movements are the most difficult to perfect.

The most powerful part of the process is that once you learn to pay attention to the simple components of your technique, you start to recognize the common principles behind power. That gives you the ability to recognize those components when you're watching or learning from someone else.

Simple, not easy!

When we can turn down some of the noise, most of life is pretty simple. We need to eat. We need to stay reasonably sheltered from the elements. We need the connection of other people. Beyond these basic needs, the rest should be a blessing!

Unfortunately, in our complex society the extras have become expectations. We often feel entitled to things our recent ancestors would have considered unimaginable luxuries.

Learn to appreciate the elegant simplicity of life and the amazing beauty in that simplicity. There's nothing wrong with wanting a better life. Once you can do that, your happiness is secure.

I try hard to base my happiness on things that cannot be taken away from me, such as my emotional and spiritual resources. I might surrender them in a moment of weakness but they can't be taken by force without my consent or submission.

Material resources can disappear in a flash; literally! I don't want to turn gloom and doom on you but a house can be hit by lightening, consumed by fire, or washed away in a flood. Cars can be wrecked. Fortunes can be lost in a Wall Street minute.

I like my creature comforts as much as the next person and I'd certainly have my mourning period if I lost them; in fact I have! I also realize as corny as it sounds, that as long as I have my health and I'm vertical and mobile I can rebuild nearly anything material. It's much more difficult to rebuild my broken spirit, recover lost love, or reconcile a damaged friendship.

Plus, if push comes to shove, I can live quite comfortably with nearly nothing. I've done it before! As long as I can see the simplicity in life I can always adjust my current expectations.

In martial arts, the basics are balance, focus and timing. It's a clean line, rooted stance and smooth connected delivery of power. It's the unity of mind and body and it's the joy of the moment.

What's simplicity in real life? How can you break personal and professional life down to the basics?

- The satisfaction of a job well done.

- An expression of love from someone you care about.

- The warmth of a nice meal shared with friends.

- The smile of a child taking her first steps.

- A moment of well-deserved recognition.

- Helping someone in genuine need.

- Sharing your wisdom or experience with someone who appreciates it.

How about earning your Black Belt? Simple, not easy!

Don't Get Kicked in the Ass!

You might get kicked in the face, but try not to get kicked in the ass!

A more politically correct way to put this might be: "Never run away…you might walk away from a fight but never run." Meet challenges face to face. You might take a beating once in a while, but the agony of defeat eventually fades. The shame of running away from a righteous fight can stay with you forever.

Of course you've got to pick your battles! Black Belt Mindset is not a "tough guy" mentality, although you've got to be tough to think like a Black Belt. Sometimes it's right and it's necessary to take a stand; other times it is right to turn the other cheek or walk away. Never surrender, but be ready at any time for a tactical redeployment!

It's never right to just stick your head in the sand. Avoiding troubles and challenges might appear to be the easiest or least painful way to go, but in reality there's no benefit in running from the good fight. The ostrich sticks its head in the sand when there's trouble but that only leaves his ass sticking high in the air ready for a good kicking!

Another wonderful fortune cookie saying is, *"Victory in battle is 10% technique, 90% courage."* Courage and spirit are often synonymous in martial arts philosophy. Spiritual resources are the most difficult to cultivate; it takes years and buckets of blood, sweat and tears to develop courage and wisdom. Take good care of these precious resources; they can be lost in a moment of weakness, indiscretion, or cowardice.

One of the reasons I initially enrolled in a martial arts program was to learn how to face up to challenges. This book isn't my autobiography so I don't want to belabor the point; let's just say that at that point in my life, self-esteem and courage were scarce commodities. I had done things that required bravery, the best example being my time as a firefighter, but unless you have awareness of your individual talents, abilities and resources, they're useless. I lacked that awareness and because of it, in my own mind, I lacked courage and confidence as well.

When you step in the ring, there's no place to hide! There's no place to hide in the dojo either. As long as you decide to stick with it, you're going to expose all your weaknesses and flaws in living color. Sometimes the color is red. Red is the color of blood, rage, and...embarrassment!

As long as you don't turn your back and run, you're going to learn to grow. Again, this works in any of life's adventures.

When I was in the 7th grade I cracked wise to a much bigger kid. I didn't know at the time that this poor guy was going through some pretty rough times at home with his parent's divorce. I saw him as kind of a bully and my only way to fight back was to be a wise guy.

I must have struck a raw nerve because this much larger young man was waiting to give me a proper ass kicking after school that day. I've got to tell you, I was in a dead panic! I had no experience at all with this kind of situation, but it was clear beyond any reasonable doubt that blood was about to be spilled…mine! I did what most sensible people would probably do in the same situation; I ran!

I ran from that fight for nearly twenty years!

Until the first time I went into the ring in front of a crowd as an amateur boxer, I carried some of the doubt, fear and genuine spiritual pain I felt the day I decided to run from my 7th grade nemesis. Shadows of insecurity still haunt me when I face a difficult challenge, although I've learned over time that this is natural. Roosevelt was right; fear is the only thing you really have to fear.

Fortunately, there's no place to hide in a boxing ring. They've even got ropes to keep you from running away! Although I'd been in some dust-ups on the street and in the bars, there is nothing quite like the feeling of facing an opponent across the ring and knowing that you stand alone to fight this fight, win or lose. It's a combination of excitement, fear and anticipation, pumped up with a shot of adrenaline.

Of course I got my ass kicked…and I was proud of it!

I had prepared as hard as I possibly could, faced a worthy adversary, and I lost. I even broke my nose in the effort, for the second time in two months. I was bruised, bleeding and battered…and I felt terrific!

My bruises cleared up in a few days, my cuts closed and my nose healed, albeit at a slightly different angle. Best of all, my pride was restored. Do you think I had the same fears the next time I stepped in a ring?

Hell yeah! But now I knew how to face and overcome those fears. After my short experience as an amateur boxer, I knew I could step into any ring and come out a better man win or lose. I learned that I could meet a challenger face to face despite any fear.

I understand now that my running away from that fight in 7th grade was really just a manifestation of my lack of self-worth. I also have memories of staring at a phone for more than an hour afraid to call a girl for a date, and I remember thinking I was the smallest guy in my school; I wasn't, I just thought I was.

Looking back I can fully understand the reasoning behind my feelings. As parents, teachers and coaches it is our obligation to train young people to have courage and face difficult challenges. It's also our obligation to provide a living example in these areas and to be there to encourage and support their efforts, win or lose. You may never realize how powerful a few well placed words of encouragement can be in someone's life for years to come, or how destructive your words can be when you discourage or demean a young person.

If you're as old as I am you may remember those ancient comic book ads featuring the "ninety-seven pound weakling." These days there's a gym in every small town in America; when I was a kid there was Jack LaLanne on TV and Charles Atlas ads in the comic books. The Charles Atlas ads would always start with the 97 pound weakling getting pushed around, sand kicked in his face, and taunted by some beefed-up bully.

Tired of getting his ass kicked, the 97 pound weakling decided to do something about his life. After "just 7 days" on the Atlas program he returns to the beach as a muscular "he-man," pops his nemesis in the face and walks away with the girl.

I can't promise you that you'll change your entire life in just seven days. My message is that perfection is a never-ending process, but having said that the first moment you decide to stop getting your ass kicked may be the most transformational and important moment in your life. Start thinking like a Black Belt by beginning this process of transformation and you'll stop allowing any further ass-kicking; physical or metaphorical!

Most of the bullies you'll encounter in life aren't the sand-kicking types from the Charles Atlas ads. Your bullies might be parents, teachers, your supervisor, or spouse. Anyone who discourages you or steps on you for their own gain is a proverbial ass-kicker. If you're getting your ass kicked, stop letting it happen.

You turn things around by completely embracing a life of excellence and continual self-perfection. You don't need to become the bully; you need to become a better person than the bully. Compete fairly and you can get ahead and feel good about it. Nice guys do finish first once in a while, and when they do their success is lasting.

By the way, Jack LaLanne understood Black Belt Mindset. He's still teaching the values of personal discipline, focus and balanced lifestyle at age 95. I don't know whether he ever earned a Black Belt, but I can tell you he still teaches the same values and commitment to personal excellence I learned from my teachers. He is certainly a Black Belt Mindset Master!

We all have someone or something trying to kick sand in our faces once in awhile. The defense is to stand up despite your fears or insecurities and finish the fight. Walking away from a fight can be an act of courage but running away out of fear, insecurity, or appeasement is a simple act of cowardice. To walk away as an act of compassion or courage requires great strength, particularly strength of character. That requires diligence in training.

If you run because of cowardice, it doesn't matter how fast you run. Your fears and insecurities will match you step for step. A Black Belt knows his greatest adversary is one's "self." You can't escape yourself by running. You can transform yourself through courage and discipline.

I don't want you to think that not getting your ass kicked means you simply learn to kick first or kick back harder! It's not usually prudent or effective to strike back in selfish anger or because of an unbridled ego; and revenge nearly always costs more than it's worth. I know the old saying goes "revenge is a dish best served cold." I don't like paying for cold food!

Here's an old martial arts song that will help you understand when it's time to fight and when it's time to walk:

"It's better not to fight.

"When one must fight it's better to injure than maim,

"It's better to maim than kill,

"For all life is precious and can never be replaced."

Learn when it's right to stand your ground or strike back, and learn when discretion is the better part of valor. Most of all, train to do what's necessary when the time comes; continual dedication to training and self-perfection is the way to Black Belt Mindset.

When Things Get Tough, Get Tougher!

"A winner never quits and a quitter never wins." This may be a cliché but it's true!

I'm passionately and deeply committed to sharing the values of Black Belt Mindset, largely because we've lost or abandoned many of these values in contemporary culture. We've become lazy, fat and complacent. In the developed world we've become a people waiting for salvation from government or worse, someone else's government. The rustic Americans of Benjamin Franklin's stories are now an endangered species; every day we're in greater danger of forever losing our ideal of the rugged individualist. We're losing our capacity for creativity and innovation, while surrendering our legacy of exploration and adventure.

We're getting soft.

Why? Is it our culture of abundance and entitlement? That certainly has something to do with it. There is a direct correlation between the effort expended to earn one's necessities and comforts, as to one's dissatisfaction for them. We've got the highest standard of living human beings have ever created and yet our appreciation for this wealth is practically non-existent.

The good news is there are still plenty of ambitious, creative people in the world who feel entitled to nothing but an opportunity and are willing to work hard to make the most of it. You're one of them. Seriously, if you haven't thrown this book out the window yet, you must agree that discipline, focus and hard work are the necessary ingredients for a happy and successful life. You may already be well developed in these areas or you may want to improve, but either way you recognize that the best rewards in life are those that are earned.

The Black Belt way is not usually the easy way. We train ourselves to recognize the natural flow of life and work with our inner nature as well as the natural cycles and conditions around us; at the same time, we recognize that a life of discipline and self-perfection is not always easy.

Neither is a life of honor and respect. There are times when it's much easier or more expedient to be dishonest, take advantage, or step on others to get what you want. Deception is often easier than telling the truth by helping you avoid pain and unpleasant consequences… in the short term.

One of the most joyous and challenging adventures in my life is teaching three to six year olds. Those of you who have children of your own, or those who work with this age group as teachers and coaches will identify with my perspective. These guys give me the most incredible moments of insight and revelation, and in the very next moment I can feel like I've just fallen into a nest of wild hornets!

I start teaching kids to stand on their own and face challenges the moment they walk on the dojo floor, no matter if they're 3 or 103. Personal responsibility, respect and honor are words my students are going to hear even if they're too young for kindergarten!

A number of years ago a parent challenged me immediately following a talk I had with my "Little Dragons" on the concept of respect. Through a sanctimonious smirk this Mom said; "I appreciate the effort, but these kids don't have the capacity to understand concepts like respect." My response was, "Maybe not, but when would you like them to start?"

Life is tough and it is never too early to start training to become tough enough to handle it. Kids love to feel strong and independent. I don't vary my teaching methodology a great deal from my Little Dragons class to my hard-core adult Black Belt class. I watch my language around the kids and maybe I goof around a little more with them, but adults like to play once in a while too!

Kids do understand a great deal about what we might consider the deep philosophical concepts of respect, responsibility and honor. They instinctively want to please and get along with one another. They don't like being isolated when they don't know how to act properly. They also have a natural inclination to help one another given the opportunity.

Most of all, they haven't been putrefied by all the ominous worries, concerns, and machinations of adult life. It's still simple to them. They understand that the reason for doing the right thing is simply because it's the right thing to do…

…especially when it's not easy!

Most wrong choices are easy ones. The wrong choice is usually the one that avoids pain or gives us access to instant gratification. It's going after the short profit at the expense of your values. It's knocking someone else down instead of putting in the work to build yourself up. It's taking from someone else what isn't rightfully yours.

It's usually tougher to do the right thing; especially when you're down and out. Why should you suffer when others are getting ahead? Why not take a short cut? Why should life be so tough?

Because it is!

The right way is not usually the easy way. It's the best way. Doing the right thing requires moral courage and a commitment to personal excellence. It requires discipline and focus; are we singing that chorus again?

It's our obligation to teach kids that life is tough and if you're going to make it you've got to be tough enough to stay in the ring. Better that the first teachable moments for respect and responsibility happen in Little Dragons class and in your kitchen, rather than in the local police station as you're bailing your 16 year old out for underage drinking and DUI.

What a miserable life, eh?

Quite the contrary! Life without challenge is boring. I've never met a truly happy person who has not faced monumental challenges. I've never met a genuinely successful person who has not experienced devastating failures. They know life is tough and they make the decision to get tougher!

Your greatest challenges are your greatest opportunities. Excellence is only special in relation to adversity. If you're never really challenged you never have the opportunity to excel; you're just average. There's nothing particularly wrong with being average, but this book is about excellence. Even an average person, and most of us are just that, can find some area of life in which to excel.

Some of the most amazing people on earth excel at simply being decent.

Now there are times when, through no fault of your own, you'll face circumstances and conditions well outside of your control. Most of the people suffering from a global economic meltdown did nothing to cause it. Some irresponsible people say you can cause floods, hurricanes and fires through negative thoughts and mindset; bullshit! Of course if you're a self-help guru selling a program to teach people how to manifest positive thought, there's certainly a marketing angle there.

Life is tough and sometimes the only way to make it is to get tougher. Whether or not you've caused your current problems, they're still yours to deal with. You may not be able to control all the circumstances and conditions around you, but you can control your response to them, if you're tough enough!

So...the trick is to become hard as nails, right?

Black Belts learn to respect the "yin and yang" of life's mysterious processes. Toughness does not exclude kindness; they go together. Without compassion you can toughen yourself into an unfeeling bastard! That's no good to you or anyone around you!

Getting tough simply means training yourself to stand up to the challenges of life and to meet those challenges with confidence and courage.

White Belt

As you start this process, consider yourself a White Belt student.

I can remember my first visit to a dojo; I'll share that in more detail with you later. For now let's stick to the feelings I had the first day I actually started classes.

I started martial arts largely to address my lack of self-esteem. I also thought it might be a good way to get in shape after several years of abusing my mind and body with drugs and alcohol. I wanted to feel good again; I had been an athlete for much of my life, including some time as a semi-pro soccer player. When I started Kenpo classes at age 25 I don't think I'd even run around the block in five years. I had a vague memory of what it was like to feel healthy and I wanted to feel that way again.

I showed up for my first class, understandably nervous and went to the changing room to try to figure out how to put on my clean white karate uniform. A uniform can really transform your mindset. It can make you feel a part of something special, part of a team.

I felt like an idiot!

Out on the floor the class started going through the basic drills, and there I was in the back row with one or two other white belts stumbling through the first punches and kicks. The first set of push-ups made me feel like I was going to puke! Now I don't want to discourage anyone from starting classes. To be honest, it really wasn't all that hard; the fact is I was that much of a mess!

In the front rows the other students were snapping their kicks and punches with impressive speed and precision! They "popped" the sleeves of their uniforms with every punch! When we started working on some self-defense techniques it seemed these guys had unlocked the deepest secrets of the ancient Masters. Of course, they were yellow and orange belt students who had been studying for several…weeks!

The one feeling I most vividly remember is that I did not want to be a white belt. I wanted to keep going to classes, at least through my introductory program, but I wanted to earn my yellow belt as soon as possible!

Today I tell new students that you earn your white belt by making the decision to leave your comfort zone and embark on the first steps of the martial arts adventure. I don't know if they believe me; it's easy to wax philosophically in hindsight. The truth is, when I started I didn't feel like I earned anything! The white belt was a gift. I wouldn't be a real martial artist until I earned that coveted yellow belt! Once you're a yellow belt you're on your way; you're really a martial artist.

In a few weeks I did earn my yellow belt. A couple of months after that I earned an orange belt. For the first time in my life I saw a logical path toward a serious goal. I wish I'd learned this lesson before I dropped out of college twice! The martial arts gave me a systemic approach to achievement:

First the white belt ranks; those were the yellow, orange and so on. I learned that these were the "kyu" ranks, or divisions, of white belt; the ranks of the beginning student.

Next in kenpo is "gokkyu," the first traditional rank. In our system this is a green belt. Now you're a serious student. At my centers we ask students accepting the green belt to look the instructors in the eyes and tell us they can make it the rest of the way to Black Belt.

This can be a great moment of transformation where you can make the decision that you're going to embrace the hard work of becoming a Black Belt; and you know you can handle it.

In another year or two you'll earn your first brown belt level. There are hundreds, if not thousands of different martial arts styles and systems in the world. There is no universal ranking; in fact, some systems don't have any formal ranking at all. Still, no matter where you go people understand what a brown belt means. It means you're getting closer to becoming a Black Belt!

Brown belt ranks are where you're "polishing the stone into a mirror." You're going to take your basic movements and techniques and work them endlessly until you're ready to test for your Black Belt. Hopefully you're also teaching by this point. The best way to deepen your understanding of a subject is to share it with others.

I don't know why, but I never really understood the importance of a logical progression in mastering a skill before I became a martial artist. It took some time after becoming a martial artist until I felt proficient at applying systemic progression to other areas of my life.

Now I look at every new adventure as a progression from white belt to Black. I see it in business, in relationships, and in every aspect of life. I saw a progression when I decided to become a speaker and when I started to write my first book.

By the way, writing a book is a great example of an adventure that can appear to be a nearly impossible undertaking in the beginning. As soon as you break it down to a series of steps, first white belt, then green, then brown and then Black, it becomes a much more manageable endeavor.

Best of all, the adventure never ends! Earning your Black Belt isn't the end of anything; it's the beginning of your life as a Black Belt.

It took me a very long time to believe I could be a Black Belt. I cannot tell you that when I earned my yellow belt that the rest of the trip was smooth sailing; not for me. I almost quit several times. I didn't have the vision of Black Belt since it wasn't my initial motivation. I did think it would be cool to someday be a Black Belt; I just didn't really believe I had what it takes.

Black Belt is a big goal. Black Belt is also a very clear goal. Whether you're a martial artist or not, you have some concept of what it means to be a Black Belt. You're probably reading this book because you want some of that!

You should set large, clear goals. However, plenty of people set big clear goals and set out with best intentions only to crash and burn or just fade away.

Here are the real secrets to accomplishing your goals:

- Your biggest goals should reflect your passion.

- Be sure you've got the material, emotional and spiritual resources you need to sustain your efforts. If not, adjust your immediate goals to fit your current resources.

- Divide your big goal into a series of progressive, attainable steps.

- Get tough enough so you won't let inevitable set-backs and failures defeat you. This is "discipline."

- Commit yourself to continual self-perfection.

- Begin…

…and that's where we are right now.

"A journey of a thousand miles begins with the first step." This is the first step!

I've just given you a white belt look at the mindset of a martial artist. Now it's time to learn how to think like a Black Belt.

A PHILOSOPHY OF ACTION

Pull up your damned pants, turn your hat around and do something. This might sound ridiculously simple, but nothing gets done unless you do it. It sounds a lot nicer if you translate it from Asian philosophy:

"In movement there is stillness; in stillness there is movement."

This philosophical statement is sometimes distorted into a justification for inaction. What it truly means, in my opinion, is that when there seems to be no motion, you're training and preparing for what's coming next. When you're in motion, you stay centered: calm, cool, and collected. That way your action is deliberate and under control, not sloppy or ineffective.

For most of us personal success and happiness is a byproduct of action. We all start with a dream, but those of us who really want to make it are doing something about it! The trick is not to balance ourselves somewhere between distraction and obsession, but to never accept ultimate defeat. Small set-backs and failures are part of the process; Failure with a capital "F" is not an option!

Black Belt Mindset **is a philosophy of action.**

I don't want to crap on anyone's golden idol, but all the positive thinking, manifesting and visualizing don't mean a thing unless you're willing to take action. Nancy Sinatra put it this way: "These boots are made for walkin'!...start walkin'!"

Everything else we're going to talk about depends on action. Black Belt Mindset is worthless unless you're willing to put some skin in the game. It takes more than a positive mindset to get where you want to go. It takes some blood, sweat and tears, and obviously a few great clichés! Since I'm running out of clichés, let's get to work.

A few years ago I initiated a philosophical debate with a student of mine. I asked him what the meaning of life was; I thought that would keep him busy for a while! He simply stated, "Pick something to do and do it well." Bam! That about sums it up, I guess! As we got a little deeper, that is, after a couple of more drinks, I realized the wisdom in what he was saying. Life is not about sitting on the sidelines, it's about playing the game.

Of course, once you're in the game you never know what the outcome is going to be. There's no risk in being a spectator; there's also nowhere near the level of reward. Action always involves risk. Once you "pick something to do" there's a chance you'll fail. There's a chance you'll suck! You might not have the talent or ability to succeed at the level you want. You might find out you're not cut out for whatever it is your heart is set on; however, you can learn something and find yourself further along than when you started.

The spectator assumes no risk. If you don't expose yourself to danger you probably won't get hurt. You also won't become stronger, wiser, or superior in any way. You will become stuck in the same pattern. Go ahead and let life pass you by without a drop of blood, sweat, or tears. You'll probably feel no pain…until you realize what you missed.

In this book, we'll talk about courage. I'll help you develop the courage to face up to risk, danger, adversity, and failure. Sitting it out or quitting doesn't require any courage.

All action involves risk, that's just the way it is. The old cliché is true: no risk, no reward! If you're willing to accept some level of risk you're on your way to some amazing adventures!

I don't teach "success in 6 months guaranteed!" Quit and you will guarantee a result: NOTHING! "Nothing ventured, nothing gained" is a fact! Nothing worthwhile is ever achieved without risk…No risk, no reward and there is nearly always regret. If you want the best view, you've got to climb the toughest mountain. The risk and danger on the hardest routes make the reward of making the summit all that much more satisfying.

So what exactly is it you should do? We will talk about identifying your talents and abilities. We'll talk about discovering your passion and following my student's advice by choosing to "pick something, and do it well!"

If you're a singer, sing. If you're a builder, build. If you're a writer, write. If you want to tap dance, do it. In fact, learn to enjoy whatever you're doing in any moment and you'll have the secret to sustained action. It helps to build this habit by doing something you truly enjoy.

Don't worry about whether you'll be good at it or not. As I said, we'll talk about passion later. I'm not really talking about that level of seriousness yet; just pick something you enjoy or something you have to do and do the best you can. You may not be any good at it yet; remember action involves risk. What you've got to do is simply get in the game.

How about trying martial arts?

Black Belt Mindset is an action mentality. I learned a lot about action from my life as a martial artist. Believe me, very few things I've done in martial arts have come easy. In my case, the frustration and difficulty I faced along the way served as great practice for the rest of my life.

This might come as a surprise to you, but earning a Black Belt is simple. It's definitely not easy, but it is simple. Earning a Black Belt requires one thing and one thing only…Practice. That's the "secret" if you're looking for one, and it works as well in business and real life as it does in martial arts.

A few years ago I was at a martial arts convention. One of the sessions featured Master Yamazaki, a renowned master of Japanese sword craft. In fact, his family was part of an unbroken line of instructors to the Imperial Family of Japan. Master Yamazaki taught most of the session through an interpreter, but he mustered enough English to tell this story, which I'll remember for the rest of my life. I'll do my best to share it as accurately as my concussion damaged memory will allow:

A young swordsman asks the Master to teach him how to become a great sword master.

"Simple," says the Master, "you only need to follow three simple rules."

"What's the first rule?" asks the student.

"Rule number one" the Master continues; "Basic practice!"

"OK, rule number two?" The Master answers again, "Basic practice!"

 Rule number three?

"MORE basic practice!"

A huge grin spread across Master Yamazaki's face and in his thick Japanese accent he boomed out…

"Like-a-Nike! Just do it!"

That's it! The same secret works if you want to become a doctor, actor, lawyer, or janitor in your local high school. All professions are admirable, provided you treat your job as a profession. That means taking meaningful action and practicing your trade as an art. Practice is really the ultimate action; it's the beginning, the middle, and the end. Practice is what transforms any action into artistry. It is the trademark of the Master.

By the way; I was a janitor. In fact, I tell any cocky ambitious Black Belt who wants to open their own school that they must first learn the true meaning of the word "Sensei." You might know Sensei as a title used for martial art instructors. Once you decide to open your own school, you quickly learn that along with the glory of teaching your venerated art, acting the sage and earning the esteem of your students, you'll also be mopping floors, washing windows and scrubbing toilets. That's the entrepreneurial reality for any newly self-employed person! You'll soon realize that the word sensei means "janitor" as well as "teacher!"

The Master never stops practicing. No matter how high-up you are in an organization, the best leaders are always the guys willing to roll up some sleeves and go shoulder to shoulder with the troops. If you're really the janitor, your art is taking care of the property under your supervision. Pride and accomplishment are not limited to particular job titles; doing your job to the best of your talents and abilities is the key to living a successful and happy life. If you're a CEO, practice being the best CEO you can. If you're a janitor; practice being the best janitor you can be.

I'll talk more about practice in the following section, Perfection. For now, it's important to realize that getting what you want out of life is a byproduct of action. The greatest action you can take is practice. And as the saying goes, "Practice makes perfect;" however, "Perfection is not a destination, it's a never-ending process."

Success comes from developing a sense of abundance in material, emotional, and spiritual areas of life. First you've got to identify and develop your talents and abilities. Then dedicate yourself to a life of action and practice in further cultivating these resources; embrace the process of self-perfection. Along the way make sure you practice gratitude; that's what keeps you focused on what you have instead of worrying about what you don't have. Repeat: "Just do it!" You'll eventually get somewhere!

Failure is the result of doubt, fear, and complacency. Doubt and fear you can manage and overcome. If you're lazy or complacent then just put this book down, go to your refrigerator and crack open a beer. There's no sense wasting any more of your time. Seriously, if you're going to get anything out of what I'm going to share with you in this book, you do have to make one very serious decision. You've got to decide that you're going to do the work. You're the only one responsible for your success and happiness.

Get to work! Your first job is to develop a Black Belt Mindset...

PERFECTION

"Perfection is not a destination; it's a never-ending process."

Tattoo this adage on the inside of your right forearm. Look at it whenever you face challenges, adversities, or obstacles. Look at it when you're not feeling worthy. Look at it when you're squinting or straining to see the light at the end of the tunnel.

You are perfect.

I know a lot of people will argue with me on that point. I understand that many of you hold the religious conviction that human beings are incapable of perfection. Let's honor that assumption for now and assume that no human can really be a perfect being. It's likely you hold that belief because human beings are fundamentally flawed, or at least incomplete. Human beings make mistakes, therefore we can't be perfect. Well, if human beings are predestined to make mistakes and you are making mistakes, then you are a perfect human being. You're doing exactly what you were born to do.

I twice had the privilege of hearing one of the most remarkable living philosophers in martial arts. Master Jhoon Rhee created one of the largest Tae Kwon Do organizations in the world and then dedicated his life to philanthropy and teaching people about the power and joy of discipline. One of the most powerful bits of philosophy I learned from Master Rhee was one of his daily affirmations:

"I am perfect, because I never make a mistake…knowingly."

That's an interesting perspective! In this simple statement Master Rhee acknowledges our fallibility, but also gives us a powerful affirmation of positive mindset. The real power is in knowing that you're going to be the absolute best you can be by doing your best not to make foolish mistakes. You're human and you're going to make mistakes, but try not to make them out of ignorance, stupidity, or wrongful intentions.

For years, Master Rhee's affirmation served me pretty well. Still, something kept nagging at me about the whole idea of perfection. Maybe I could get through life pretty well without necessarily thinking I was perfect. Maybe I could find a way to reconcile this deficit between knowing that I could never really be perfect, while still finding the motivation to try to be more so.

All it took was a simple semantic shift. The further I studied the wisdom of ancient martial artists, the easier it became to recognize a theme. Every story was about the journey, not the destination. The Master's search for perfection was never finished and always brought him back to some fundamental truth, some clear and basic level of understanding.

Forget perfect; let's focus on perfection. Instead of looking at perfection as an objective, try looking it as an action. Transform perfection from a noun to verb; change it from a place to a process. If perfection is a place, then it's a specific point in time or space where this ideal can be reached. Can you possibly imagine a place or time in human existence where you will be completely without faults, doubts, fears, regrets, or desires? HA! There's the rub! Life doesn't work that way; unless you're completely delusional!

What if you just let go of the idea that perfection is a destination? Embrace perfection as a process and everything changes. As soon as you can accept it as a process, it becomes permanent and you don't have to hold on to anything. Just allow yourself the awareness that the process of perfection never ends; it's continual.

Borrowing from Buddhist tradition, it's significant to recognize that the Buddha teaches us, in order to be a perfect human being, you just have to be. The Buddha also recognized that this state of human perfection during the course of human life was transient, fleeting and difficult to hold on to. Indeed, the only way to hold on to this state is to completely let go or become unattached to the human conditions of desire, longing, and attainment. The practice of Samadhi, or intense meditation, can encourage you to reach this state of human perfection, while maintaining the understanding that it's an interminable process.

Now you're continually engaged in the process of self-perfection. Every day holds incredible opportunities for transformation and growth. You become aware of these opportunities because your mind and heart are open to new experiences and resources that will further your process of perfection.

As you engage in the process of perfection, you continually develop skills, talents, abilities, and knowledge that make you a more revered individual to yourself and to everyone around you. You increase your value in the world. You become a more productive worker, a more effective leader, a stronger parent, and a more involved member in the community. Don't expect fireworks; this process is subtle and the changes you experience are sometimes only recognizable in retrospect. Over time, you advance in life and become more like the person you want to be and move closer to your vision of success and happiness.

A tradition commonly used in Japanese martial arts is the practice of "kata." Kata is a set of choreographed movements used to train, exercise, and practice martial arts techniques. The most direct translation of kata is "form." A more meaningful understanding to a martial artist is "correct movement." A kata is really an exercise to perfect your movements, while striving to develop unity with your mind and body. If you delve deeper into kata practice, you can develop an understanding of the application of each movement. It's the application that's commonly understood to be the "secret" of the form.

In Zen traditions there are puzzles, or questions, that have no solutions. These puzzles are called a "koan." A kata is a lifelong koan; you're never going to finish perfecting a kata. Embrace perfection as a process and the kata isn't an end, but a means. If you assume that there's a point in time where the kata is perfect; the trip is over!

Isn't it the same in real life? I don't care if you're talking about personal life, business or professional life it works the same way. When are you the perfect janitor? When are you the perfect CEO? When are you the perfect parent, friend or lover?

Embrace the process. Whenever you're in the process of perfecting yourself, you are in a moment of perfection. If perfection is a process, it's not a destination; therefore, you're always there…Perfect!

Perfection isn't some person you're going to become; it's who you are…Perfect!

The confusing thing is that in order to embrace perfection as a process, you've got to realize that you're never going to be "perfect." Stop worrying about it! Stop thinking about perfection as some kind of carrot and stick proposition. You know the old story about the proverbial donkey with a carrot strapped to a stick just out of his reach. He keeps moving toward the carrot and that's what gets the proverbial cart moved.

You're not a donkey. You know that if you look at life this way you're never going to get that damned carrot. After a while you wise up and quit. You've got to pull the cart because you actually want to move the cart. Carrots are okay, but the more you need the carrot the more dependent you are on the reward instead of enjoying the journey. When you learn to enjoy the journey, you'll begin to enjoy the numerous rewards that are offered every step of the way.

Don't believe me; try this for yourself. I'm not perfect; I've just learned to enjoy the process. Most days this makes me a much happier person. I'm happy, but never quite satisfied. Maybe that's why human beings can't be "perfect" in the classic sense. That's also maybe why we've evolved to be industrious, creative, and resourceful!

Perfection depends on the following three major characteristics of Black Belt Mindset:

- Excellence

- Discipline

- Focus

EXCELLENCE

Too many people think excellence is for the chosen few. That's just dead wrong. You might think that you're average and that excellence is a quality that describes someone better than you. Change your mind. Excellence is not only attainable; it's your personal responsibility.

Excellence means reaching the highest levels of performance, production, and creativity that you can achieve. Compare yourself to others and you'll always find people better or worse than you are; that's incidental. Compare who you are today to who you were yesterday; that's a meaningful comparison.

Everyone can be excellent! You'd be right to question that statement. How can that be if excellence is a quality that describes the highest levels of performance? There are the best, then the rest; right? It's not about being "better" than someone else; it's the other guy's job to be his best; it's your job to be your best. In some area, in some expression of your talents and abilities you can excel. Excellence is a choice, not an accident.

I make two promises to my martial arts students and only two:

1. If you're willing to do what it takes to get to Black Belt you'll be able to do anything you want within the scope of your talents and abilities.

2. You'll learn how to recognize and develop your talents and abilities.

That's it. You don't have to be better than everyone else to be excellent. You've got to identify your unique talents and develop them to the best of your ability. You've got to commit yourself to becoming a better you every day of your life. That's what excellence is all about and nobody else can do it for you.

The fact is that every person on this planet has some talent or ability in which he or she can excel. Other people can help you develop.

They can teach you, coach you, encourage you, and hold you accountable, but the work is yours alone. All excellent people use mentors, coaches, teachers, and trainers; they know it's a part of the process. They also know that when you step in the ring you're on your own. Your trainer is in your corner to coach you, give you a different perspective and sometimes to throw ice in your trunks; nevertheless, you're the guy who has to take the shots.

The Black Belt has undeniably become a universal symbol for excellence. The renowned "Six Sigma" business program co-opted this symbol to represent the highest levels of training in their system. Once people find out I'm a Black Belt in martial arts they have a certain expectation that I've mastered the fighting arts and assume that I've dedicated myself to a lifetime of training and self-perfection. They'd be right in that assumption provided they understand that the Master is always a self-directed work-in-progress....

"Perfection is not a destination, it's a never ending process."

The pursuit of excellence has no final reward. The reward is in the doing. It's just like climbing a mountain. The climb can take hours, days or even weeks. You only spend a brief moment at the summit enjoying the view; then it's back down to get ready for the next climb.

We're treading water in an ocean of mediocrity. You can only tread water for so long before you're rescued or you decide to swim for shore; otherwise you'll drown. Too many Americans today are waiting for rescue; it's time to start swimming. I'd rather drown giving it my best than waiting for a boat that might not ever come.

And that's what excellence is all about; it's a commitment to being your best. Anyone can be average, in fact, most people are. There's nothing terribly wrong with being average provided you're satisfied with that. The problem comes when too few decide to rise above being average to do the hard work necessary to excel.

American society has reached a very dangerous place in time. Mediocrity, complacency, and apathy is too often tolerated and even to a degree, rewarded. We've got too many people treading water and not enough people willing to man the boats.

The pursuit of excellence is too often seen as unobtainable at best, corrupt at worst. Too many people think that the only way to the top is by stepping on the necks of others. Too many people also think that excellence is measured only by acquisition of tangible rewards, especially money. Nowhere is this problem more apparent than in business.

While it's true that some people who dedicate themselves to excellence can become financially wealthy, that's not always the case and it's not usually necessary. People who dedicate themselves to excellence will usually feel successful. I won't pretend to define anyone's individual success, but I do know that to feel successful and happy you need to have a sense of abundance, or a feeling of having "enough" in three key areas of life: material, emotional and spiritual. How much is enough in each area is completely up to you.

No, the authentic rewards for excellence can't be tallied on a balance sheet. Dedicate yourself fully to the pursuit of excellence and your rewards are knowledge, experience, and wisdom. You'll develop self-confidence and you'll learn to recognize and develop your talents and abilities to your fullest potential. All of that can be leveraged to produce material wealth, as well as personal and professional success; however, these are also resources that transcend the limitations of material wealth. If your pursuit of excellence is sincere, these resources can survive hardship and help you rise above periods of adversity and even poverty.

Anyone pursuing the Black Belt in martial arts understands that excellence is about being the best; the best that you can be. It's not about being "better" than someone else; it's about being better than you were yesterday. It's about being better tomorrow than you are today. It's about practicing your art, your craft, or your chosen profession to further perfect your talents and abilities no matter how long you've been at it.

Still, it's naïve to think that bettering a competitor isn't sometimes part of it. I hate platitudes and I can't stand teachers who cash-in on the abundance craze in the sense that everything you need is readily available to those who simply have the proper positive attitude. It is absolutely true that everything you need to achieve your personal vision of success and happiness exists in abundance. A positive mindset and a sincere expression of gratitude will open your mind and heart to the possibilities and opportunities available to you in any given moment; at least much more than a negative mindset will!

It's also true that there are circumstances and conditions outside your control. You've got to transform your positive mindset into positive action to get anywhere. You can tread water, or you can start swimming. Better still, you can learn how to build and sail a boat.

Excellence is sometimes about being better than the other guy, but don't waste a minute feeling guilty about it. It's his job to be his best. Your pursuit of excellence does not take anything away from anyone else, provided you respect personal and societal ethics and positive values. In fact the opposite is true. When you dedicate yourself to excellence you become a greater resource to other people. You become a leader, someone who can be counted on to produce and increase the possibilities for others in your business, your home and your community.

People who are jealous, fearful, or guarded about anyone else's pursuit of excellence are weak. This kind of weakness breeds a disabling culture of entitlement; or even worse, it can breed dictators in society and business. Weak people try to protect whatever false sense of control or temporary satisfaction they can cling to. They're more likely to take from others rather than contribute to the common good.

Dedicate yourself to excellence and you're much more likely to become a contributor. I believe that's your responsibility and obligation, but I don't worry about it much, simply because excellent people tend to share more than mediocre people do. Part of what they share is the knowledge, experience and wisdom that they use to develop excellence. Excellent people tend to want to help others become excellent. Just keep in mind that there's only so much you can do for the other guy. Commit yourself to excellence! Let the other guy worry about being excellent himself. When everyone is committed to excellence everyone improves. In business, the result is that an entire market segment rises in value. In an organization, the result is more creativity, productivity and profit.

I used to worry that if people heard me talk about being excellent that I'd offend someone. Nobody likes a cocky loudmouth. I learned that to be excellent you've got to cultivate self-belief and confidence. It took me a long time, but I finally got kicked in the groin enough to realize that if I didn't start with self-belief I wasn't going anywhere.

I started playing semi-pro football as a 44 year old rookie. Many of the guys on the team were young, cocky, and loud about it. I remember thinking at first that if they were so great, why weren't they in the NFL? As I started to become friends with these guys and learn about their lives, I quickly developed a new appreciation for their confidence. Some of these guys had the talent to play in the NFL. Some of them played Division I college football. One got kicked out for selling drugs to the coach's daughter, while another joined the Navy to support his young family. Stuff does happen!

It took me a while, but I started to realize that to any one of these guys, his sole expression of excellence was this football team. Real life might be kicking him in the nuts, but here on the football field every Saturday he was the best. To be the best you have to believe it. To believe it, you've got to tell yourself you're the best and keep reminding yourself when you forget. Believe me; it's easy to forget after some 240 pound fullback puts his shoulder under your chin and turns you into a human Pez dispenser!

Positive self-talk has become a science. Now we've got PhD's writing books that outline the psychology of positive self-talk. My football brothers learned it on the streets as a survival mechanism. Here they were teaching a middle-aged rookie suffering from a life-long self-esteem problem how to talk the talk that helps you walk the walk.

A placekicker has a very close relationship with two other guys on the team, the long-snapper and the holder. This unit has to be rock solid in timing and execution for a successful field goal. Our unit developed a ritual: We'd come out to kick and my guys would say "Where's it going?" My job was to answer "Through the pipes!" Then we went to work to get it there.

My holder was one of those guys who given the right breaks might have had a shot at the NFL, or at least at a good college football career. He was always telling me I was the best kicker in the league. Once he got me saying it, and once I started believing it, we led the league in scoring for two consecutive years.

Now was I really the most talented kicker in the league? Who cares?! The point is that the act of believing in excellence led to action. We became excellent as a unit because we believed we could; then we did the work to make it happen. Saying you're the best does not diminish anyone else; it's the other guy's job to be the best he can be. When everyone is working toward personal excellence, the power of the team, organization, or community expands exponentially.

Fair competition develops excellence; at least it should!

"Be one with your enemy." That's an interesting and useful bit of martial arts philosophy, but what the hell does it mean? It means that your enemy, your competitor is part of you. To the warrior, the enemy is necessary to complete your understanding of your "self." You need your enemy to fully test and appreciate your skills, talents and abilities. Without a worthy opponent, a warrior is never truly tested and really doesn't know what he's capable of. How can you measure excellence without a challenge?

So, your enemy or competitor is really your best partner. A formidable adversary helps you develop your best skills, talents, abilities, and mindset. You should appreciate your enemy, and give him your best effort in battle. In the boxing ring the champion needs to be tested by increasingly better competition; you can't become a champion until you fight the champion! You can't stay the champ unless you fight the best contenders. Your enemy becomes a necessary and valuable part of the champion's development toward excellence.

In the dojo you're not helping your training partner with a half-assed effort. You've got to give your best in order for your partner to improve, while you expect the same in return. It is the same deal in life and business; and just like in the dojo, you can also share your knowledge, experience, and wisdom to help your partner, or competitor, excel. Of course, you've got to be strong to have the confidence to share on that level. Again, excellent people tend to be more sharing. They know that sharing doesn't diminish their value, it increases their value!

I sometimes catch people working on self-defense drills with a half-hearted effort. I offer to teach them a magic trick. I'll take the student who was practicing the defense and throw a punch at the same mediocre speed and intensity I caught them at. Then I'll say, "Watch this!" I put my hand on the students shoulder or head and tell him I'm projecting "qi" (chi) into his body to make him faster. Then I tell him to get ready because I'm going to knock his head clear off his shoulders. I like to add some pizzazz to the show by asking another student to stand behind to catch the head when it pops off.

Now before you think I'm a real creep, I know I'm not really going to hit my student and most of the time they don't think I'm going to either! Well, they might wonder for the first couple of years. Anyway, I take a stance, give a yell, and throw a full speed punch aimed right at my student's nose. They block the punch every time!

"See!" I declare, "Magic! This guy just got 100 times faster!"

OK, I will admit I adjust the speed of the punch to the student's relative ability; but it's always a faster and more powerful punch than his partner was throwing. The student always rises to the occasion. You can't develop excellence without facing a challenge that tests the limits of your talents and abilities. The best help you can offer others is to give them your best effort, particularly when you're trying to help partners, peers, and subordinates.

Be confident, not cocky. Confidence is built on knowing your abilities and having faith in the reasonable chance of your desired outcome. Cocky is just blowing air to get other people to notice you. Excellence demands some degree of confidence. Confidence is developed through training.

Muhammad Ali was often accused of being cocky. He once said, "Some people do say I'm cocky, some say I need a good whoopin', some say I talk too much, but anything I say I'm willing to back up...," and back it up is exactly what he did! He trained as hard, if not harder, than any other fighter in his class: physically, mentally and spiritually.

We've all got a stake in our culture of mediocrity. You're never going to change everyone; there are people who are satisfied with mediocrity. Some of us aren't and it's up to us to become excellent. Do it fairly and with honor; not by stepping on others, but by making greater strides with yourself.

The most genuine reward you'll earn by embracing excellence is freedom. Excellence is the key to self-reliance and independence. With excellence comes choices and people who dedicate themselves to excellence have more options.

Ultimately, excellence is the path to power and that's what being a Black Belt is really all about. To unlock this power you've first got to learn how to Think Like a Black Belt, and the first step is discipline...

DISCIPLINE

Discipline is the foundation of excellence. Discipline is the most important component in developing power and effectiveness. Discipline is the most essential characteristic of Black Belt Mindset.

Here's a wonderful definition:

Training expected to produce a specific character or pattern of behavior, especially training that produces moral or mental improvement.[1]

Discipline is the action of developing the habits and characteristics that will move you toward your personal vision of success and happiness. Nothing is more important to living a life of constant self-perfection. Discipline keeps you going when motivation is low, adversity is high, and frustration is seemingly your only companion.

When I'm talking about the Dynamic Components of Personal POWER, people often ask me which component is the most important. I always say discipline. That's the key component to all the others. You can't maintain motivation, focus, balance, and timing without discipline. You can't improve yourself without discipline.

Simple, not easy!

Discipline is training, but it's also the result of training. Focused training develops you into a disciplined person. Anyone can train, but you'll only fully understand discipline when you reach a point where you can't imagine life without training.

Earlier I identified 3 components of failure:

- Fear
- Doubt
- Complacency

Discipline is the solution to all three components of failure. Through discipline, you can find courage to face your fears, reduce doubt, and eliminate complacency.

[1] discipline. Dictionary.com. The American Heritage® Dictionary of the English Language, Fourth Edition. Houghton Mifflin Company, 2004. http://dictionary.reference.com/browse/discipline (accessed: July 08, 2009).

Most new martial arts students say they want to be more disciplined. That's a great goal! Over the years, I've asked hundreds of people in and out of martial arts if they consider themselves disciplined people. I'm always shocked to hear how many people say they lack discipline. I've heard this from janitors and I've heard it from CEOs. I've heard it from reformed criminals and from military officers!

I've found through experience that most people are much more disciplined than they realize. Almost everyone has some area where they are extremely disciplined whether they know it or not. The trick is to open up the mind and heart to understand discipline, be able to recognize it in yourself and others, and to be able to access or develop a training regimen that will continually improve your self-discipline.

Before we go much further, I've got to say I have met people that genuinely have no self-discipline. Fortunately, they're the exception, not the rule. Sometimes it's just because they've never been taught how to develop discipline. That's what a lot of people come to the martial arts for; to learn how to develop discipline. Most of the time it's an easy fix; it's just a matter of giving them something difficult to do, encouraging them to do it, and then pointing out to them that they did it and how!

Some people have been so discouraged or beaten down by others emotionally that a full reconstruction job is what's needed. This is what happens to abused children and battered women, though they're not the only ones susceptible to this kind of emotional trauma.

Sometimes alcohol and drugs can rob people of discipline; this happened to me. The danger of substance abuse is that it robs you of the very thing you need to transcend the condition: discipline. When I found martial arts, I was recovering, or at least I was ready to recover from a life of drug abuse, self-perceived failure, and a complete lack of self-value and worth. Martial arts gave me a structure and a system of recognition, in which I started to recognize my own personal development for the first time in my life. I may be a little biased, but it's a great place to start!

No matter what trauma, conditions, or circumstances you've faced in your life you can turn it around through discipline. You can take the first step at any time no matter where you are in life. You've got to do the work yourself, but there's absolutely nothing wrong with reaching out for help. In fact, the very act of recognizing that you need help and asking for it is an act of self-discipline. Asking for help is sometimes the first step in becoming an independent and self-disciplined person.

Unfortunately, there are some people who genuinely don't want to do anything to improve. They don't want to do the work. These are the walking dead; the complacent, lazy bums and leeches that are perfectly happy being consumers without contributing a damned thing to the world. These are the vampires, the human sponges; these people are a waste of food and they make me want to puke.

That's pretty harsh; sorry, that's how I feel.

My compassionate side still allows that if the couch potato will summon just enough energy to drag his fat ass off the couch and into one of my beginner's classes; I'll commit myself entirely to his salvation. If he genuinely wants to be a slug, let him rot.

The fact is that complacency is contagious. It's an infectious disease and in my opinion lazy people should be quarantined. Stay away from them so you won't become infected! You know some of these folks; they're the emotional vampires. They always complain but never offer a solution. They see all the faults in the world but never do a damn thing to change them. They take but never give. They live on entitlements and never express gratitude for any help they get.

Still, there is a cure even for the worst of 'em! The cure is discipline.

Even the most lazy, complacent human sponge can become a disciplined person. No matter how little discipline you have right now you can improve and eventually become a self-disciplined, successful and happy person.

How?

One punch, one kick, and one step at a time.

Substitute a punch or a kick for any other activity you can think of. It might be learning your first chord on a guitar, your first dance step, or doing your first 5 minutes on a treadmill. It might be learning your first phrase of Spanish or taking the first section of a real estate broker's program. It might be enrolling in one adult ed class at your community college or asking your boss to spend a few extra minutes with you to find out what you can do to position yourself for a promotion.

Just pick something and do it. That's it. No psychological bullshit; just do it.

Now if you've legitimately experienced some of the more severe conditions I talked about a few minutes ago, you might consider getting some psychological counseling. There's nothing wrong with asking for help; in effect, this might be your first step in discipline. Any counselor that earned his sheepskin will soon help you realize that you've got to do the work. Good counselors, teachers, gurus, and shamans are tour guides of the mind. You're the one that has to do the walking!

I'm going to use martial arts to provide an example; martial arts are about discipline. The very definition of art is centered on discipline so any art is a great tool to develop discipline.

As I said, most people I've met are much more disciplined than they give themselves credit for. It's a quirk of our culture that sometimes the most disciplined people get the least attention and recognition. Remember the great message from the classic movie, "The Wizard of Oz." The Scarecrow, Tin Man, Cowardly Lion, and Dorothy had everything they were searching for; they just needed a challenge and some tangible recognition to help them develop awareness and cultivate the great gifts they each had all along. I don't think Toto knew what the hell was going on, but he was a dog, not a person!

Martial arts works because we provide a challenge and a tangible point of recognition for accomplishment. It's that simple.

At one point in my career I was waxing all too philosophical and decided to get rid of all the belt ranks in my schools. I was studying Tai Chi at the time in another system that didn't have formal rank recognitions. They recognized people as instructors at some point, but all of it was far less formal than the Japanese ranks I inherited in my Kenpo practice.

I asked some of my students how they'd feel if we got rid of the ranks. We had a ten rank system starting at white belt and going through yellow, orange, purple, blue, blue with a stripe, green, green with a stripe, three levels of brown and then the Black Belt. The story I heard was that Kenpo originally had just four ranks: white, green, brown and black. In fact, the legend went that you were given a white belt to close your jacket and that over time and training it became green, brown, and eventually black. We don't wash our belts, so I can only imagine what these early Kenpo guys smelled like if their ranks were dependent on the rancid condition of their belts!

I was just about ready to go back to this traditional ranking when one of my students stopped in to tell me he didn't think that was a good idea. He asked me if I knew how much his yellow belt meant to him. I said I didn't; maybe I was becoming a jaded old bastard! I admit I was kind of surprised; this student was someone I really looked up to! He was a federal judge; a man of incredible accomplishments and esteem in my eyes! In fact, I had asked him on a couple of occasions what the hell he thought he could learn from me; a two time college drop-out, reformed drug abuser and ex-punk rocker!

This student told me that in his job, he could go years without any significant positive recognition. Week after week his job was to put people in jail; some of them he felt would be no better for the experience. He saw the worst of humanity and I believed him when he said he seldom got a thank-you from anyone he was sending up the river! Earning his yellow belt marked the first time in years that he was recognized simply for doing a good job. He told me how important it was to all the students, particularly the adults, to be recognized for showing some progress in Kenpo. They faced the challenges I threw at them, did the work and frankly they deserved the recognition.

I knew at that moment that I'd never eliminate our ranking. One punch, one kick, and one step at a time these students practice a craft that's difficult and sometimes even painful to master. They struggle through frustration, criticism, correction, conditioning, and practice. They come in day after day and embrace the process of perfection in themselves and through the practice of martial arts. Unlike the monks of ancient legends, most modern students also do this while raising families, holding down jobs, and participating fully in the rigors of real life.

This is discipline. When you're recognized for your discipline and training this creates a powerful positive reinforcement emotionally and spiritually. The human psyche responds to positive reinforcement with feelings of joy and self-worth. That in turn provides motivation to continue the journey. That's discipline.

The funny thing is that I recognized this student as an extremely disciplined person though he didn't see himself that way. That's why I failed to see the importance of the recognition. I figured this guy is a federal judge, he went to law school, what could a lousy yellow belt given to him by a middle-aged misfit who spends half his days in pajamas mean to him? The recognition helped this student and the others recognize their own discipline or at least reminded them what discipline looks like. That's important.

You don't need to be a martial artist to develop discipline, (but you won't catch me talking you out of it!) Anyone can do martial arts and there are now hundreds of different styles from gentle Tai Chi to full contact Mixed Martial Arts and Kickboxing. There's something for everybody!

If martial arts aren't your bag, just be sure whatever activity you take up has these two essential discipline building elements:

- Progressive levels of challenge.

- Recognition of progress.

There is tremendous value to participating in some kind of formal program with a skilled guide or instructor, but you can design your own discipline program. You can create progressive levels of challenge and some system of recognition even in a self-directed activity. The highest levels of personal discipline transcend recognition. In martial arts we say it this way:

"The student must someday become his own teacher."

Let's say you're taking a night course in real estate sales. Reward yourself for completing each section of the program. You might share your accomplishments with a friend with a celebratory dinner at certain points; and of course, you'll want a nice party when you pass your real estate exam!

You can create your own program of self-improvement. Put together a reading list of books that will help position you for your next promotion or help you start your own business. Keep a checklist and reward yourself as you finish each book. Make up a diploma and sign it when you finish your self-designed program.

One caution about self-directed discipline building programs: Don't reward yourself too soon! An effective teacher or Sensei knows when the student is ready for praise and reward, that's part of the art. Set clear goals or objectives and reward yourself only when you reach those goals.

You might be learning guitar and your goal is to work through a complete lesson package. It would be tempting to buy yourself a new guitar halfway through, but it won't necessarily make you a better musician. You should save your reward until you really reach your goal. The wonderful feeling of playing your new guitar at the moment of achievement will anchor that feeling of accomplishment and will help sustain you through future challenges.

Discipline is not brain surgery. It's hard work, focus, and staying on task. It's working through frustration, disappointment, and discouragement one punch, kick, and step at a time.

Pick something that challenges you and go for it. Just do it. Don't worry about where you're going just yet, just keep punching and kicking one step at a time. No matter how it feels at the time, every single step, every action, every act of a disciplined person brings you closer to your goals.

Repeat.

Soon you'll be a disciplined person. Eventually, you'll become a Master...

FOCUS

You can't force focus. It's useless to try and force yourself to concentrate. Focus is really a process of letting go; it's a matter of turning off the noise and letting your mind do what it does naturally. When you turn off the distractions you operate at peak efficiency and the mind naturally settles on the task at hand.

Of course, turning off the noise is more easily said than done! Sometimes it's physically impossible to eliminate distractions at a specific moment that demands your full attention. You can train yourself to "tune-out" distractions, which requires some work and some understanding.

Focus is a seriously misunderstood trait. Too many people confuse focus with obsession. Obsession is focus gone bad, focus without regard for balance. Focus is simply your ability to commit your attention to this moment. Focus means being right here, right now. As with much of what we're talking about, it's simple, but not always easy.

Focus is the quality of Black Belt Mindset that enables a martial artist to break boards, bricks, and other people when necessary! Focus is the concentration of power, free from distraction that allows every ounce of power and force to be directed to one critical point of impact. While it's fun to break boards, there's not a lot of practical use for that particular application of focus; but if you develop this kind of focus, you can apply it to any task you want.

Focus is important on two major levels. First, you want to cultivate the ability to stay on task at any given moment. Secondly, focus is your ability to keep your mind on a substantive and important long-term goal. I'll cover long-term focus more when I talk about perseverance. For now it's just important to know that focus is really being in the moment, it's just that sometimes this moment might last a while.

We live in the golden age of multi-tasking. The problem is that multi-tasking is a myth. The human brain isn't capable of dealing with two conflicting thoughts or ideas at the same time. Dr. John Medina and many other neuroscientists have gathered some pretty compelling data in that area.

It's also true, however, that in our incredibly noisy and fast-paced world people who can deal with the noise and confusion are pretty valuable people! Multi-tasking is really the ability to shift focus quickly from one target to another and back again. The lag-time problem most people experience happens when you try to come back to the original train of thought. People who can do this quickly and successfully are the people we say are good "multi-taskers."

Throughout history we've admired people that are incredibly skilled in a multitude of interests. Two of my greatest heroes are Leonardo DaVinci and Ben Franklin. We called them "Renaissance Men." They had the ability to cultivate many different interests and express themselves in a variety of ways, while staying focused on a particular endeavor in the moment. They weren't scattered, they were very focused men. They were simply able to stay focused on what they were doing in the here and now; then move on to the next project.

You can do this! You can train yourself to shift your attention quickly from one task or subject to another and back again. In the greater scheme of things it's pretty expensive emotionally and spiritually to sustain this pace for any significant length of time. That's why it's so important if you're operating at this pace to take some time outs and let the brain rest for a while.

Before we talk about how focus works, let's beat this obsession thing until it's dead.

Focus is being in the moment. It's being fully engaged with what you're doing here and now. Obsession is focus out of control. Obsession is focus without balance; it's focus without any awareness or regard for what's happening around you. The line is clear but thin, which is why it's so easy to cross it at times. When you're moving in a positive direction, that's focus; when your focus is damaging you or the people around you, that's obsession. That's why the **Black Belt**

Mindset depends on balance as a mitigating force.

When you become so hyper-focused on one thing so that other significant parts of your life suffer, you're no longer focused; you're obsessed. It's easy to slip into a state of obsession; it's like the proverbial scalded-frog. You don't notice the gradually rising heat. What was once healthy ambition, drive and focus, can suddenly be recognized as obsession when your wife leaves, your kids are calling from jail, or your regular check-up turns into bypass surgery.

Extreme examples? We all know people in one or more of these pickles. Most of them never saw it coming.

Focus is one of the Dynamic Components of Personal Power. Power is applied effectively through the components of balance, focus, and timing. Without balance, the whole thing collapses. Obsession drives us to build expensive houses in stupid places like flood zones, perennial hurricane targets, and places prone to brush fires and landslides just to have a nice view. Obsession transforms ambition into greed; it's the difference between profiting from your talents and abilities, and profiting by destruction and exploitation. Obsession causes us to cling to youth rather than enjoy the miraculous gift of age. So how do you maintain focus without becoming obsessive? You simply have to be sure that any given moment is in balance and harmony with other important areas of your life. Balance the material, emotional, and spiritual areas of your life by creating a plan based on building wealth in all three areas.

There are times when it's effective or even necessary to focus more in one area than another. You might feel compelled to take on a second job to keep your home and family intact during a tough economy. The trick then is to make sure you dedicate some quality time for family and friends, so when it's time to be with the kids you are fully engaged and focused in that place and time.

When one or more key areas of your life suffer, and the material, emotional, or spiritual resources are in a state of scarcity, you're going to be in trouble. This is the time to take a step back, take a deep breath, and install a course correction. Poverty is expensive; it cannot be sustained for long. Emotional and spiritual poverty are far worse conditions than material poverty; but poverty in any area can lead to poverty in others.

If you're experiencing poverty in one or more areas, focus on a solution. To the best of your ability turn off the noise and distractions that are keeping you in that state. Here's the technical part of your focus program.

Focus is a product of two actions. They can sometimes work independently or sometimes it's best to combine them.

1. Concentrate completely on the task at hand.

2. Let go of any distractions; turn off the noise.

Both actions require practice. "Simple, not easy," means that this stuff should be so painfully obvious that you're either slapping your forehead with the palm of your hand or you're ready to throw this book out the window. Still, even though you know the common sense of the issue there are still times when you'd rather just bull your way through a problem, enjoy some distractions (even when they're not always healthy) and take your chances so you'll live to fight another day.

It's up to you. All of this starts with a decision and it's all your responsibility.

I'll start with concentration; it seems to be the most obvious place to start, doesn't it? The problem is that forced concentration takes a lot of energy and usually can't be sustained for very long. It's a state of tension. It's force against force, and that's always exhausting.

Here's a quick exercise to test your powers of concentration. Gently close your eyes...not yet, you've got to finish reading this paragraph first! Anyway, gently close your eyes and start counting. Keep counting until any thought or picture pops into your head. Every time a new thought or picture comes to mind, start your counting over again. Do this for about two minutes.

How far did you get? Let's analyze what it might mean depending on how far you were able to count:

1-25: Nice job! You're actually aware of the various thoughts and distractions that came into your mind. A lot of people aren't! If you had a hard time getting past even a low number, you realized that the human mind is constantly developing new thoughts. It's part of how we sense the world around us. You've taken the first step toward developing deeper levels of focus.

25-100: You still have a reasonable sense of awareness, but ask yourself if you might not have noticed some thoughts that came and went. Maybe you were authentically focused on the counting and you tuned out the noise of other thoughts. Maybe you're a Shaolin monk!

100 up: Get out of here! Either you really are a Shaolin monk, you're lying, or you just weren't paying attention! It's extremely difficult for most people to get to this count without having some thoughts or distractions creep in. What usually happens is that because counting is such an automatic practice, you may have gotten lost in the counting and never noticed the thoughts that were coming and going. Take a couple of minutes right now and think about the thoughts you probably had while you merrily counted away without even noticing that you were still counting!

There aren't any good or bad scores here; it's just an exercise to see where you're at and to point out how difficult it is to truly quiet the mind. There are people, Shaolin and Tibetan monks being some of them, who go to great lengths to quiet the mind for long periods of time. What they've learned over centuries of practice can help us a great deal toward honing our concentration skills and learning to become more focused.

Primarily, they learned that focus is largely a matter of turning off the noise. It's our nature to be drawn to distractions; that's probably what kept us alive when we were still the main course for saber-toothed tigers. What we call multi-tasking is important to success in business and professional life these days. What we've got to do is develop control over when we're going to move from task to task and increase our ability to return to the task once we deal with a distraction.

There are also times when it's important to stay focused without distractions. Writing this book is a great example. I can't concentrate on writing when I know the phone is likely to ring or I'm juggling several other tasks during a busy day. It's important to this process to create a space and time where I won't be distracted or interrupted, and I can't allow myself to feel guilty about it.

Let's talk first about removing distractions, then we'll talk about getting back on task quickly.

To really focus on an important or demanding task you've got to turn off the noise. This takes some discipline and practice. For some people it means very rigid scheduling by specifying time away from distractions. Other people create a noise-free space where they can escape to work on something without interruption.

When I say "noise," I'm not just talking about honking horns, ringing phones, or screaming brats; I'm talking about mental noise too that may pull you from the object of your focus. In fact, sound can help you concentrate as long as you pick sounds for your environment that help you concentrate. Think of "sound" as being harmonious with your focused mindset and "noise" as something that bugs you.

To me there are three major areas of distraction:

Actual noise: these are the honking horns, ringing phones, and screaming brats.

Annoying people: Anyone who is distracting me and pulling me from my focus. These people could be detractors, those with negative attitudes who think whatever you're doing is stupid, a waste of time, or doomed for failure. They might also be "emotional vampires" (More about this in a few minutes).

Negative mindset: Anything that creeps into my psyche that pulls me from my task, such as self-doubt, questioning the value of the task and guilt that I might be taking time away from something more important.

Let's knock out the easy stuff first. When you're working on something important that requires your complete focus, just make sure you get away from the noise. Turn off the phone, shut the windows, and lock the kids in their rooms! (Just joking about the kids…) Too many people use this kind of distraction as an excuse, and excuses are focus-killers.

Everyone can find a quiet place or time. If all else fails, nearly every town in America still has a public library, and there are still specialists there that "shush" anyone who attempts to distract focused people. I often drive to a nearby park and pick a place where there aren't other people, and then I sit down and get to work. If you've got to stay and tend to the family, schedule times after the kids are in bed to do your focused work.

Turn off the phone! Not only does the phone make noise, there's often an annoying person at the other end of the call! The fact is, those calling you are making the call when it's convenient for them. You know that's a fact; you do the same thing. If you're really expecting an important call, don't plan on working on something that requires your immediate focus. Most of the time, there's nothing so important going on that you can't just let the caller go to voice mail and deal with it later.

I offered this advice to a friend one time who said she was afraid that if she turned off the phone, she might not be available if someone in her family died. I asked her if she was expecting impending, disastrous news. No, she was just worried that if it happened, she'd need to know! My sensitive reply was that if someone was dead, couldn't they wait? Dead people certainly aren't going anywhere fast!

Annoying people are a little more difficult to deal with. You can't just tell everyone in your life to leave you alone all the time, but you certainly should tell them to leave you alone some of the time. Of course, you may work for some of the most annoying people in your life, and you might be related to some of the others! Attention to sensible scheduling will allow you to avoid distractions from annoying people, most of the time.

As I stated earlier, you really need to be aware of "emotional vampires." These are the people who will drain your mind and body of energy to feed whatever they can't seem to find in their own lives. Emotional vampires might be the compulsively negative people in your life. They might not even ask for much, but spending a morning with one of these vampires can wipe you out for the rest of the day. Negativity can be contagious.

If you're a decent and compassionate person, you no doubt have at least one emotional vampire somewhere in your life. They could be at work, in your family, or in your circle of friends. You don't have to be mean or insensitive; you just have to establish clear boundaries. Do not base your generosity and time on the vampire's requests, but on your ability and willingness to give it. This is not selfish, it's essential.

So, give them a clear message that you need some time. If they don't respect your wishes, tell 'em to get lost! Life is too short to waste it on people who just want to sap you of your emotional resources. If you loan a deadbeat friend some money and he doesn't pay you back, you can earn more money. When someone steals your time, it's gone... forever.

Up to this point we've been talking about focus in regards to a particular task. Now let's talk about focus and apply it to life as a whole.

Successful people focus their time, energy, and resources by developing clear goals. They make a plan and use that plan to stay focused. There are numerous tricks and techniques to keep you focused on your overall goals and objectives. For instance: Vision boards, business plans, personal financial plans, family meetings, and schedules can all be useful techniques that keep you focused on future goals.

You can use formal systems, or you can scratch out a plan on a pad of yellow-lined paper; however, the important thing to remember is that it's much easier to stay focused when you commit your plan to a tangible format.

Remember that success is a product of abundance in all three key areas of life: material, emotional, and spiritual. There's a time and place to focus on each area. Be present in the here and now.

There are also times when life will, by necessity, fall a little out of balance. There are times when you've got to suck it up and focus on material needs. There are times when people in your life need you and you've got to put aside other things to focus on emotional life. Focus in the moment but keep your sense of relative balance. Also remember that mindless focus becomes obsession.

Nowhere is this more evident than in material life; it's too bad when someone is so focused on the pot of gold that they miss the rainbow. Spouses, friends, partners, children, and lives are lost in the pursuit of the brass ring. Consider this: If your toys are stressing you out you've got too many toys, or they're too expensive. I don't pretend to judge anyone else's vision of success and happiness, but I know that plenty of rich people are a mess and most of them shouldn't be. Money can't buy happiness, but it sure as hell can take care of a lot of life's problems! Pursue money and toys at the expense of emotional and spiritual resources and you're setting yourself up to be on the "Where are They Now" tour. If your toys make you happy, great! If not, get rid of 'em.

Material life can be one of the most difficult areas to keep in balance. When times are tough you've got to focus on making enough money to keep food on the table and a roof over your family's heads. When times are desperate, it's easy to put aside all emotional and spiritual needs and focus completely on the material.

Don't.

Of all forms of poverty, material poverty is the simplest to deal with. I'm not diminishing authentic hardship; been there, done that. No matter how desperate you become, including worrying about where your next meal is coming from, you can do something about it. If you destroy a relationship it may be lost forever. If you lose your sense of spiritual connection it's difficult to recover; many people don't.

Let's simplify the process; just remember that simple isn't always easy. At all times, stay focused on creating an overall sense of balance and harmony in your life. Take care of yourself in body, mind, and spirit. Do what you can to stay healthy so you'll be more valuable in the lives of the people you care about.

Focus on maintaining balance in the material, emotional, and spiritual areas of your life. Take some time daily to reflect on where you are and to appreciate what you have in each area. Gratitude is a powerful technique for bringing your focus back to what you have, rather than losing yourself to despondency over what you're lacking.

Meditation is the most powerful technique I've ever found to help me maintain focus on life balance. Gratitude is the most powerful part of my meditation practice.

Despite my many years of practice and study in martial arts, I'm not Damo. I'm not the Dalai Lama or Gandhi; I'm an American kid born with all the impatience and arrogance that is our birthright. I've had to learn to develop a simple practice I can do every day to help me maintain my focus. Here's what I do:

> I get up and say thank you. That's it. I just say thank you for the people and things in my life. That's how I stay focused on what resources I have. No matter how rich or poor you are, you're working with what you have here and now. I especially make it a point to remind myself of the blessings I have for my talents and abilities. That's a tough thing to do for someone who spent most of my life with no self-esteem! I can create my vision of success and happiness with the talents and abilities I possess, which can never be taken away from me. I can surrender them, but they're mine to lose!

> I do a short set of stretching and breathing exercises called "Qigong." My regular daily routine includes a couple of hours of exercise, but

doing this simple set helps wake me up and gets my circulation going. Doing it first thing in the morning assures that no matter what happens to my schedule, I've at least done a minimal amount of physical and spiritual exercise.

I then sit down and breathe. I turn off the noise and just let thoughts come and go. I let go of distractions, and when a distraction comes up, I simply turn my attention back to my breathing. An ancient trick is to do a little self-talk: "Breathing in I'm aware that I'm breathing in. Breathing out I'm aware that I'm breathing out." I call this my "non-directed" meditation. I'm not worried about goals or objectives. There is no aim to this mediation. I'm just sitting and being a human being for a few minutes.

Next, I do a "directed meditation." I spend a few minutes simply thinking about what I want to achieve today and in the long run. I do positive self-talk; I tell myself I have the talent and ability to accomplish my goals. I get myself mentally prepared to face the day.

If I have time, I read for about a half-hour. I read philosophy, self-improvement, or business books that will help me focus on my continual search for self-perfection. If I can learn just a little bit every day then I'm way ahead of the curve.

This simple routine has helped me stay focused during some of the darkest days of my life. I wish I'd known how simple it was much earlier in life; so it goes! I'm grateful I had wonderful teachers and that I live in a time when I can access wisdom from nearly any time and place in human history.

A lot of people challenge the idea that developing focus can be this simple. Screw 'em, it is! Focus is above all, a decision; simple, but not always easy (note the recurring theme!) You've got to decide you're going to let go of the distractions and do what you need to do. It's the same whether you're focused on your morning ritual or a specific project at the office.

It's not easy to turn off the distractions because:

- Sometimes they feel really good!

- They keep us from feeling the pain of a task or job we don't "want" to do.

- Procrastination is the warm blanket that insulates us from disappointment.

You've got to pull up your trousers and make the decision that you're going to let go of the distractions. Develop your own morning ritual to practice letting go of distractions and allowing your mind and body to focus on goals, objectives, and positive outcomes. Practice gratitude as often as possible; gratitude always helps you focus on abundance and purpose.

Above all, turn off or tune out the noise and your mind will naturally settle into a focused state; that's our natural mindset. Make a decision to let it happen.

CONFIDENCE

S ome people "got it;" the rest of us have to build it.

Confidence has a close cousin: faith. You're going to need both to achieve success and happiness. You're going to need confidence to even recognize success when it comes. You're going to need faith to transform that success into a lasting experience, which is really how you develop happiness.

Confidence is nothing more than a reasonable certainty that you can accomplish what it is you set out to do. Confidence is an emotional resource. You can measure it with some degree of accuracy. Confidence is based on experience; every time you face a challenge and overcome it, you build confidence.

Faith transcends experience. Faith is a spiritual resource that is difficult to measure or sometimes difficult to find at all. In a moment of realization, faith can swell your chest until it feels like bursting and charge your entire nervous system with electric tingling as you somehow know with absolute certainty that everything is breaking your way. The next moment it's gone and the only reason you know it was there at all is because of an overwhelming sense of loss comes over you as doubt and fear, all too eagerly, take its place.

I guess you could say that confidence is the tangible expression of faith at times, which is really important when you're leading others. It's a fact that nobody is going to follow you if you're not confident. We'll talk much more about leadership later, but it's important to note that all successful people are leaders. I'm not saying you've got to be a senator, president, or CEO. I'm saying that to accomplish your goals you're going to need the help of other people. My friend, Marsha Petrie Sue, says it best: "You're the CEO of Y-O-U!" You're the leader of your mastermind team. You've got to show your supporters you know what you're doing and most of all that you believe in what you're doing. They can't always see, recognize, or understand your faith; they can easily see whether or not you have confidence.

The good news is that both confidence and faith can be developed and practiced.

Confidence is probably the most recognized characteristic of Black Belt Mindset. It's a common observation for people to notice a certain level of confidence and self-assurance when they meet a martial artist. Lots of martial artists confidently advertise "self-confidence" as a benefit of training in their programs. Most adult students tell me martial arts training improves their self-confidence, while parents always tell me that their children become more confident through martial arts.

It would be nice to tell you that I've always been self-confident and that one of the most important reasons I teach is to share that important quality with others. That would be a lie. It's true that self-confidence is one of the most important qualities of Black Belt Mindset. It's true that helping other people find self-confidence is one of the most important reasons I teach; however, it's also true that for much of my life I didn't have any.

I've sat alone in a crummy apartment wondering if I'd ever meet someone to share my life with. I remember being laid-off and wondering how I was going to find work. I've put myself into crippling debt. I've experienced depression; in some of those moments I've turned to drugs, alcohol, and have even considered suicide.

Many of you might ask how anyone could possibly consider taking his own life. Having looked in the mirror at someone considering suicide, I can tell you that for me the reason was a complete lack of confidence. Why would anyone want to be with me? Why would anyone want to give me a job? What was I worth to anyone? What was I worth to myself?

That level of depression is directly related to a loss of self-worth, and that's often a result of a lack of self-confidence. When you lack the faith and confidence in yourself to change your circumstances the world becomes an empty and angry place. It seems as if everyone around you shares in some fantastic secret that you're not worthy or capable of understanding. It's very easy, and somewhat comforting in a moment like this, to simply resign yourself to a life of horrible mediocrity; or to just end it all.

That's a truly dangerous moment. Some people will finish the job; others will condemn themselves to a slower, perhaps even more painful process of self-destruction through drugs, alcohol, and complacency. Of the three, complacency is the most dangerous and addictive drug.

There's really only one way out. To survive any addiction, experts will tell you the first step is to accept complete responsibility for your current condition. Look in the mirror and admit you've got a problem.

It's a painful admission to look in the mirror and realize that you simply don't value yourself. The fact I realized is that there weren't any outside forces keeping me from happiness and success; that force came from within. Like most people in this condition, I had plenty of reasonable explanations for feeling the way I did, and some of those reasons were legitimately imposed on me by others, particularly when I was young. I had to learn the difference between an explanation and an excuse.

It may be that your father was an unfeeling bastard and your lack of self-confidence is the result of his mistreatment or lack of encouragement. It's also true that from this moment forward the rest is up to you. An explanation is not an excuse; you've got to accept personal responsibility for who and what you are, here and now, if you want any hope of transforming your life.

I don't remember feeling at the time this moment of enlightenment was the first step in building self-confidence. I only realized in hindsight that I experienced this moment of realization, which truly took place over the course of a year or two.

What I do remember now is that I started to realize that whatever was happening in my life wasn't someone else's doing. I learned that there is no "The Man" and I didn't work for him. I couldn't get a date because I wasn't sharing my light with the women of the world. I was desperately seeking someone who would put up with me as I was. Today I wouldn't wish that version of me on anyone!

The first step in building confidence is learning to recognize and accept even the smallest success or the smallest step forward. At the same time, you've got to accept full responsibility for making the changes you want in life. Whether you caused your present situation and circumstances or not, they're yours to remedy.

Start to recognize some small successes and you start to realize that you have some value. Build on this value and you start to share your value with others. The people around you then reflect back this value in a desire to be with you.

Part of this process is opening your ears, eyes, mind, and heart to what's going on around you. You may not always get the feedback you desire from everyone you hoped for, but there is most certainly someone for everyone, as long as you're open to it.

I was amazed and a little ashamed when I started to realize that I was important and valued in the lives of some of the people around me. They'd been shouting it all along; I wasn't receptive.

So…

You've got to be open and receptive to the people around you and understand you have value in the lives of others. The more you improve yourself the more value you share with others. Still, the ultimate responsibility for creating your self-confidence is yours and yours alone. Be open to the encouragement of others and at the same time, know that it's up to you to do the work.

Self-confidence is somewhat related to self-esteem. "Self-esteem" is cliché, overused, and doesn't really describe what you need. It's not about holding yourself in "higher regard," it's more about recognizing your true worth and value in the world. You can develop self-esteem to a degree just by practicing self-talk exercises and regarding yourself highly in your own mind. Worth and value are reflections of what you contribute to the people around you. The more important you are in the lives of others, the more self-worth and self-value you feel. Make sure you're listening when others tell you how much you mean to them.

Before we get too far ahead, I better clarify what I mean by faith. Faith, like other spiritual resources and practices, can be religious, but it doesn't need to be. Faith is taught in most religions, but it's not often explained very well. It's sometimes used to control people by teaching that faith is a gift from God and only accessible through complete acceptance of a certain doctrine. Faith is part of your wiring whether or not you're religious, you believe in God, or you accept or even know about any particular religious doctrine.

Daily life depends on your faith in the possibility of good things coming your way today; otherwise, why face it?

Faith sometimes transcends experience. Faith can be the simple hope that everything will work out for the best. Faith is trust in the good nature of other people or a sense that you're connected to a purpose that will somehow reveal itself if you stay the course. You can have faith and hope even without any rational reason for it. It's sometimes just a feeling; and sometimes it's all you've got! You may still believe in a positive outcome, despite the fact that every experience you've had and every neuron in your brain is telling you you're up shit's creek without a paddle!

Faith is also sometimes very elusive. You may have every reason to believe that things will work out for the best, but you just can't seem to hang in there until it does. Maybe this is a survival mechanism. Maybe a little doubt and pessimism is also hard-wired into us to keep us from happily leaping off cliffs like a bunch of ecstatic lemmings every time we feel great about something.

Faith is necessary to move forward toward your goals, maybe even just to get up in the morning, but there's certainly good reason to avoid obsessive or blind faith. Develop authentic faith based on acceptance in the essential goodness of human nature. Why should you believe in the goodness of human nature and the probability that your life has meaning? Because you have faith!

And that's the secret to becoming a Black Belt: constant, never-ending self-perfection and development of your personal power. Believe in yourself and your ability to apply that process and you can achieve success…and happiness.

We started this argument by emphasizing the importance of personal responsibility, right? It's right to accept responsibility for a failure; it's self-defeating to identify yourself as a failure just because you happen to fail. Your business may fail, but if you've given it your best you are not a failure. That is a critical distinction you've got to make in order to preserve some semblance of sanity. As long as you avoid internalizing the idea of becoming a failure, you can take whatever is left after a failure, including new knowledge and experience, and get on to the next adventure. Your venture may not have survived, but you've survived and may even be wealthier in emotional and spiritual, if not material resources. You may be even better prepared for success than you were before you failed.

As I said, successful people do sometimes fail. They've just learned how to pick themselves up, dust themselves off, and start all over again. They've developed the confidence to take another chance, and that's extremely important. When you've been up against it you can quit. I won't lie, quitting is an option. You can quit, or you can keep going. Only one of these choices guarantees a predictable result. Quit and you know what's going to happen: nothing. Keep moving forward and everything is at risk. You're putting chips on the table. These chips are money, reputation, self-esteem, and maybe even your health.

Any and all actions carry an element of risk. It's important for your mental and physical well being to understand your tolerance for risk at any given time. Confident people seem to be more comfortable with risk.

The best situation is when your confidence is rooted in training, preparation, and experience. You're reasonably sure about producing a desired outcome because you know you're doing everything you can to produce that outcome. Your confidence is fortified by past successes and by the confidence you have that even if your effort fails you've got the ability, courage, and will to survive any loss and keep going.

Confidence isn't a self-assured knowledge that you're going to win all the time; it's knowing that whether you win or lose you're going to survive and grow. It's knowing that if you get knocked down seven times, you'll get up eight.

One of the most powerful moments in my life was the day I earned my Black Belt. Looking back now, it seems to me that before that day I was constantly struggling with a lack of self-esteem. After that accomplishment I can now believe in myself. I knew from that day forward I could accomplish anything within the scope of my talents and abilities.

What changed that day?

Nothing!

I wasn't magically transformed the moment I strapped on that Black Belt. The transformation had been going on for a long, long time! That moment was the product of buckets of blood, sweat, and tears. I now understand that any moment of accomplishment is a predictable outcome, as long as you face challenges with courage, persevere through moments of doubt, failure and frustration, and develop faith that every step in the journey is a meaningful and important part of where you're going.

My confidence doesn't come from wearing a Black Belt; it comes from having earned it. I'm not sure where I'm going next, but I know I'm going somewhere. I can say with utmost confidence that I'm going to continue to face doubt, fear, pain, and frustration. I can also say I now have the confidence to face all of that and more. Most of all, I'm confident that I have value in this world and it's my responsibility to share that value.

POWER

My first book was all about power. I'll focus here on the bare bones of power and how important it is to Black Belt Mindset. You can't become a confident person until you start becoming powerful. I know; I had it backwards for a long time.

First I want to clear up some bullshit ideas people try to force on others about power. Number one is that you don't have access to all the power you need to accomplish whatever you set out to do. You have access to all the power you'll ever need, but it's up to you to actually generate that power to accomplish anything.

Power is simply this:

Your ability or capacity to act or perform effectively.

That's it. It's not about control; that's the currency of the dictator. It's not about some secret technique or practice; anyone can cultivate effectiveness and generate power. I'm giving it to you here because power is about developing yourself to be more effective; it's about the continual process of self-perfection. The more you dedicate yourself to this never-ending process, the more power you generate. The more powerful you become the more valuable you are to yourself and others. Face it, weakness is not a very useful or attractive force. If you want to be effective you've got to generate power. If you want to multiply that power and attract the people you need to help you succeed, you've got to share it. That's authentic and effective leadership.

Let's quickly hit the basics. If you want to know everything I've learned about power, read *Dynamic Components of Personal POWER!*

Like I said, there are people ready to feed you all kinds of crap about power or tell you why you can't have it or don't deserve it. After 40 plus years of believing their crap, I was able to condense most of the problem down to "The Top 5 Lies About Power."

1. Power corrupts. No it doesn't; people corrupt power. Power can be used for benefit or destruction; the choice is yours.

2. Power is just for the powerful. Well then, how did they get there? Developing power is a process that can start with the barest minimum of resources. It's your responsibility to develop your power. Start now.

3. Money is power. No it's not; neither is knowledge. Money and knowledge are valuable resources you can use to increase your power, your capacity for effectiveness. It takes action to transform money and knowledge into power. If money and knowledge were in and of themselves power, all rich and smart people would be powerful and no stupid or desperate people would be. Is this true?

4. Power is control. No, power is your ability or capacity to perform or act effectively. Control is imposing your will on others. Power is the currency of a leader; control is the currency of a dictator. Which one do you want to be?

5. You can't get it! The worst lie of all! Every human being has the capacity to develop tremendous personal power. Within the scope of your unique talents and abilities, your potential is unlimited.

Sometimes people tell you these lies because they're trying to protect their own feelings of being powerful. Let 'em waste their energy; it doesn't work. You can't protect power and the only way to expand power is by sharing. That's why the most effective leaders are people who cause us to see our richest potential and encourage us to get there.

Most of the people who tell these lies aren't trying to knock you down, at least not maliciously. Parents, teachers, coaches, and managers sometimes tell these lies in an attempt to protect you. People who care about you don't want to see you fail or suffer; they don't want to see you embarrassed or frustrated.

Sorry, that's the price! Find people who are willing to help you off the mat and back into the fight. Power is your ability or capacity to act or perform effectively. If someone is trying to prevent you from developing power, get this person out of your life. You want the people who will stand by you as you do what it takes to become a more powerful and effective person. This is a long, arduous, and painful process. You need people who are going to stick by you when you're winning, and when you're losing.

So how do you do it? How do you become more effective and more powerful? Here's the short version; let's call it Power 101:

Power is your ability or capacity to perform or act effectively. The one thing you can always control in your life is the ability to cultivate power. You can expand your ability, or capacity, to perform or act effectively at any time in any place. You don't need money, knowledge, or fame to increase power. Expanding your resources is part of developing power. So, you can start with little or nothing and take one simple step and become more powerful.

Power needs a source and the source of all human power and energy exist in Body, Mind, and Spirit. I call these three components the "Energy Triangle." To be a more powerful person, you've got to nourish your Body, Mind, and Spirit. You can summarize these components simply by saying you've got to take care of yourself!

Before we go any further, I want to mention one of the greatest cop-outs is when you say you can't spend time on yourself because you've got other people to take care of. Here's an easily understandable example: Let's say you're turning into a fat slob because you won't take the time to exercise when you've got to get your kids to Little League, your work schedule is a bitch, and your wife is complaining that you're not spending enough time with her.

Here's the alternative:

Don't exercise.

Continue to gain weight.

Develop heart problems or diabetes.

Become a statistic. (Think "preventable" illness or death!)

I used to be soft about this stuff. A parent of one of my students stopped in one day and told me he had just gotten some bad news from his doctor. He already had diabetes; now the doc was telling him that if he didn't get some exercise he'd be headed for serious heart trouble within months.

When I first started teaching martial arts I might have been a pushover and just offered some words of sympathy. Over the years I've learned that being blunt is often a greater act of kindness than being blandly sympathetic. This guy had been watching his kid in my classes for a couple of years now and like many parents, once in a while he'd say, "I'd love to be doing that." I'd always say, "Let's get you started to-night," which he usually laughed off.

This guy was the straw that broke the Sensei's back. I said, "Look, you've been watching your son in class for two years and telling me you'd love to try it. I'm giving you a free six-month program; start this week."

What do you suppose he said? What would you say? He said he didn't have time. I asked him how much time he'd have for his wife and kids if he was dead in six months! I guess I'd crossed over to the dark side; and to this day I've never come back!

If you don't take the time to take care of your health what are you to the people around you? If you have kids, it's your responsibility to set a good example. Do you want them to be obese and have to deal with illness that can be easily prevented? Do you want them to be tired, miserable and depressed? Or, would you like them to emulate you by living a healthful, energetic and joyful life?

If you're sick due to your own negligence you're a burden to your family, friends, co-workers, and society in general. About 80% of all health care expenses in the United States are due to conditions that could be prevented with a minimum of exercise and reasonably sensible lifestyle choices.

If you're sick, you won't be shuttling your kids to soccer games; they'll be rolling you to their games with an oxygen tank strapped to your wheelchair!

Did I scare you? Good! A bit of an exaggeration? Maybe, but life is hard enough without you adding problems to your life that can be easily prevented just by taking some time to take care of yourself. Next time you see an obese person rolling down the street in a state subsidized electric wheelchair with the requisite oxygen bottles, ask yourself if this could have been prevented. There are conditions and circumstances beyond our control sometimes, but that's the exception, not the rule!

Your mental and spiritual health is just as important as your physical health; it's just a little less obvious when mental or spiritual health is starting to slip. Nobody gets divorced because of what happens in one day. Only in the most traumatic situations does someone fall into a depression in a matter of hours or completely lose all faith and hope because of one incident. In the vast majority of situations, emotional and spiritual poverty comes about over an extended period of time.

An emotional and spiritual scarcity is usually a process caused by erosion. Taking time to care for your emotional and spiritual well-being is just like your physical exercise program. You've got to pay attention to how you're feeling and if something isn't right, you've got to take action to correct it before the problem becomes acute or dangerous to yourself and others.

Nurture your Body, Mind, and Spirit and become a healthier and happier person. Take care of the sources of human energy and you'll have the resources you need to develop your Power and ability to act effectively.

You develop Power through the components of Motivation and Discipline over Time. I call these components the "Kung Fu Triangle." Kung Fu is a Chinese term that means achievement through effort. You might translate this idea as simply "work." You've got to work to develop power and to create a successful and happy life.

Motivation is pretty easy to understand; it's whatever gets your heart and mind singing, and whatever gets your feet and hands moving. At the beginning of nearly any process, motivation is a relatively abundant commodity. You might be excited to start a new job; a couple of years down the road you might be saying this same job sucks, you're stuck in the rat race and you want to get off the treadmill.

Think about what happens every January. How many people set New Year's resolutions to lose weight, find a new job, quit smoking, or make a substantive change in life? Most of these resolutions fail before the ice melts in the champagne buckets! Why?

To succeed in any goal your motivation must be internalized. Motivation is successful when it's based on clear, attainable objectives instead of emotional reactions to current conditions. You also need to know you've got the resources to start and sustain your efforts. You might be inspired to action by a certain external motivator such as, a speaker, book, movie, person, or some kind of revelation; but to be successful you've got to internalize your motivation based on your goals and resources. Motivation can start with emotion but you've got to make it tangible if you want the best shot at success.

The process of transforming motivation into sustainable action is the process of Discipline. This process is very important, so much so, that I've already devoted an entire chapter to it in this book; it really deserves its own book. Discipline is developing the habit of doing whatever it takes to attain your goals. Discipline is an ongoing process that requires a lot of energy, attention, and nurturing. That's why you've got to take care of Body, Mind, and Spirit!

All of this takes Time. Power isn't just a flash of enlightenment and bam, instant success! Generating power is a continual process of self-perfection and self-improvement, which takes time.

How much time does it take to develop power? How much time do you have?

The fact is, this process never stops; it just repeats. You usually start with motivation; motivation starts to wane and discipline takes over; keep going over time and you start enjoying some success, which in turn generates more motivation. Keep this process going over time and you will find yourself moving closer to your goals. Or, you might find that you've discovered some new goals and adventures that you never imagined when you started!

Quick review, then you'll have a good working knowledge of power:

The sources of all human energy and power are:

Body

Mind

Spirit

You've got to nourish all three to have the energy you need to generate power.

You generate power through Kung Fu:

Motivation &

Discipline over

Time

Once you generate power you want to apply it efficiently and effectively. Use the components of the "Power Triangle."

Balance

Focus

Timing

We touched on balance in the sense that a happy and successful life is when you keep a relative and dynamic sense of balance in the 3 key areas of material, emotional and spiritual life. Keep that in mind. Balance also refers to keeping a sense of grounding; what martial artists call "rooting." It's about keeping your feet under you!

Some of these concepts are easier to understand by looking at their opposites. We sometimes don't realize we're happy until something makes us sad. Balance is not always as noticeable as the feeling of being out of balance. When life starts spinning out of balance you might feel lost, depressed, anxious, nervous, exhausted, or angry. When life is in-balance you usually just feel good!

For a fighter, balance is the foundation for delivering a punch or kick with power and effectiveness. Remember power is your ability to act effectively. You've got to have a solid foundation; otherwise you can throw a lot of energy at a target and still not produce any effect. Don't confuse exertion with power. You can work awfully hard without producing any results; that's exertion, not necessarily power.

Start with balance. Keep your feet under you as you move. In real life, just like in the ring, the target is usually moving. That's why I call these concepts the Dynamic Components of Personal Power. Life is in constant motion. It's a dynamic process and you're much more effective if you can keep moving; but you don't want to be tripping over your own feet! Pay constant attention to the importance of balance.

As I stated about Focus, you've got to be on target. Your greatest successes come when you concentrate your power and energy on a specific target, goal, or objective. Good focus keeps you from wasting power and energy, while instead you can conserve it for the next move.

Almost everyone has seen a demonstration featuring a martial artist breaking boards, concrete blocks, ice, or some other seemingly indestructible material. I can remember what was going through my head the first time I broke a board. If you've never done it, it's probably the same thing you'd be thinking. I knew I could do it; I'd just watched my instructor do it. I was wondering how much it was going to hurt. I was wondering if I'd break my hand!

A five year-old kid can break a pine board. I've taught dozens of kids to break a board. There isn't any particular trick to it. No, we don't saw a groove on the back-side of the board. We don't bake the boards in ovens; though it is true that seasoned boards break easier than freshly cut boards. We do sometimes use smaller boards for kids, but that doesn't make the surface of the board any softer.

The barrier you face the first time you break a board is a simple one. Boards are hard. Concrete is even harder. You think of these materials as unbreakable, since your house is likely built of boards. It's a little disconcerting to think that some bald maniac could start punching holes in your house!

Most of you also know that if you tapped a one-inch pine board with a hammer or a hatchet, it would split without a drop of sweat. You might also not have any problem stomping the same board with the heel of your boot. You know it's not going to hurt! But you're not going to hit this board with a hammer or the heel of your boot; you're going to smash it with your hand. Add to the mix that your Master just told you that you've got to hit it dead center; focus your mind there! Most of us break our first board with someone else holding it; that adds another factor, particularly if you watch someone attempt a break before you and the holder flinches!

Remember that focus isn't something forced; it's a process of tuning out the noise. A radio doesn't receive a single frequency; it takes in the whole spectrum. The tuner selects which frequencies it's going to process depending on how you've set the dial. You've got to do the same thing with focus.

Your partner is holding the board steady. You've got other students around you watching; some of them are nervous because they haven't had their turn yet! Your Master is watching you; maybe your boyfriend decided to come watch this particular class to watch you make an idiot of yourself! You start thinking about how hard the board is and how relatively soft your hand is. You wonder if your partner is going to move. You wonder if you've really trained enough to be doing this yet. Too many minds!

The real trick is to tune out the noise. Look at the center of the board. Visualize a point just beyond the board, take aim, and let go of any other distractions. Then just wind up, scream a blood-curdling kiai, and punch it through! You hear a crack, you realize it was the board and not your hand (most of the time!) and you're done. You just proved to yourself that you're harder than the board.

Now you can continue your training with two boards, or more. You can move up to concrete, ice, or whatever else you can find. If you want to play piano later in life, I wouldn't worry about trying to destroy everything at your local lumber yard. Just be satisfied knowing that with focus, you can take a barrier you once thought impenetrable and you can punch right through it.

Doesn't it work the same way in personal and professional life? I've got to tell you that for me, breaking a stack of boards still seems easier than the sick feeling I had staring at the phone attempting to call a young lady for my first date! I've broken my hand trying to break boards and blocks; the broken heart is a far deeper pain!

Tune out the noise; let go of the distractions. Focus on the center and punch through. If it helps, yell!

Timing is the final component of the Power Triangle. Pun intended: It takes a lot of time to develop good timing. Muhammad Ali could float like a butterfly and sting like a bee; that's great timing. It took him more than a week or two to develop this timing.

All these components are interdependent. To develop good timing, balance, and focus you've got to practice. This requires motivation and discipline applied over time. This requires a healthy energy source in body, mind, and spirit.

Timing takes the longest time to develop. If you came to one of my martial arts classes you'd understand balance and focus relatively quickly. It still takes a long time to develop mastery in balance and focus, but with timing there is no intellectual short-cut. In other words, you could improve balance significantly just by bending your legs; try it! You could improve focus simply by aiming at a specified target. Developing timing takes hundreds or thousands of repetitions. As an instructor I could give you a sequence, but I can't do the work for you. You've got to internalize timing through practice.

The person who commits to this practice becomes a Master.

Timing also involves understanding the movements of your opponent. A weaker, slower fighter can beat a stronger, faster opponent with great timing. Timing is the product of training and experience. You can borrow a little wisdom and experience from your teachers, coaches, and trainers; but ultimately, you step in the ring on your own. The better your training the better your timing is going to be in the ring. Experience, coupled with constant self-perfection, really gives you the edge in timing.

As I write this book, I'm still playing semi-pro football. I'm nearly 50 years old. I'm playing against kids whose mothers I might have dated after their first divorce! This year I'm specializing completely in kicking. I've played other positions, but my interest in football has always been primarily kicking. I was questioning whether I was still a real football player until I heard this great line in the movie "We Are Marshall." Mathew McConaughey, playing the coach, is working with a kicker who is standing around after he puts the ball in play. He asks the kid why he's standing around and the kid says, "Coach, I'm just the kicker." The coach replies, "Son, once you kick the ball you're a football player!"

That's a great way to look at training. At 49 years old I'm playing against younger, usually faster, often much more gifted athletes, and at 185 pounds I'm not usually the biggest guy on the field! I will not be out-trained! If you're going to beat me, you're going to do it heads-up. I refuse to lose due to a lack of preparation. I put the time in at the gym, training on my own and learning my skill. I pay attention, do the reps, and develop the timing to give me the chance to beat a better athlete one-on-one.

Sometimes it works!

Consider the same thing in your personal and professional life. What is your competition doing right now? Are they studying new product lines and benefits? Are they practicing their sales presentation or developing a new trade skill? Are they continuing to develop the skills they already have and doing the reps that will give them great timing?

Defeat at the hands of a worthy opponent is manageable and even sometimes honorable. Self-defeat is inexcusable.

Study the competition. Understanding your opposition helps you exploit your good timing. Compare yourself to the competition; learn to recognize your mistakes and weaknesses, and know where you can make room for improvement. Distinguish your enemy's strengths and weaknesses, and how to exploit these attributes as well. Sometimes our greatest strengths are our greatest weaknesses.

Balance, focus, and timing give you the ability to apply your talents and abilities effectively and efficiently. This is power.

The "secret," if you want one, is "practice." Commit yourself to self-perfection as a never-ending process and enjoy yourself along the way. I've never met a happy person without power. I have met plenty of powerful people who weren't happy, but I've never met a happy person who wasn't powerful.

I said I'd come back to this, so...

Earlier I identified the Top 5 Lies About Power. One of these lies was "money is power." You could substitute knowledge, fame, or goodwill. You've heard these lies:

Money is power.

Knowledge is power.

Fame is power.

Goodwill is power.

Money, knowledge, fame, and goodwill are not power. Power is your ability or capacity to perform or act effectively. Money, knowledge, fame, and goodwill are valuable resources you can use to develop power; your efforts to generate power often produce more of these resources, but in and of themselves, none of these are power. Power comes from how you decide to recognize and utilize these resources.

You recognize the resources at your command through gratitude. Take a look around you and start giving thanks for everything and everyone in your life at this moment; no matter how much or how little you have right here and right now! If you're on the low side right now, give thanks for whatever you DO have. Let go of any attachment to what you don't have; for the time being, that's not important. Wherever you're heading, you've got to start right here, right now with what you have.

As you develop your material, emotional, and spiritual resources you become more powerful and you've got much more to share with others. Ultimately, the purpose of power is to bring greater value to yourself and to the people around you. The ultimate act of power is sharing; helping others develop remarkable skills and become "powerful."

When times are tough it's too easy to lose sight of these concepts. Just remember this:

Stay focused on developing yourself and making yourself more powerful. Nobody is attracted to weakness. Black Belt Mindset is a mindset of power. With power you are more valuable to everyone around you. You're a more productive and effective member of your family, your organization, and your community. That's how you attract the people who will help you reach your goals, particularly when your goals are aligned with theirs.

Embrace power. Too many people are afraid of power, or they just don't understand it, or they're just too damn lazy or irresponsible to accept it. A powerful person is a leader. A leader, as we'll explore in detail later, is not someone who controls through fear, intimidation, or restriction; a leader is someone who attracts willing followers. People are attracted to power and confidence. It's your responsibility as a successful person to be a leader, and that means learning to be comfortable with power.

There are plenty of books about the philosophy of power. My focus is to try and simplify the concept of power so everyone can develop it and apply it. I want you to understand, embrace, and share power; hopefully much earlier in life than when I started.

One of the great blessings of living in our time is the access we have to the treasure of world knowledge, wisdom, and philosophy. I'm sure most of you have at least a mental list of people, living or long gone that you'd like meet. I call the people on my list the "Dream Team." These are people I admire. These are the people I'd love to call on for advice and counsel. Much of their wisdom is available in books, which is important because most of my "Dream Team" is either inaccessible for the time being, or quite inaccessible because they're dead!

It took me a while to understand the authentic meaning of power; and even longer to learn to embrace power and to accept the responsibility that goes along with it. One of the great teachers who helped me in this adventure is Lao Tzu. I'd love to sit down with him; I've got a lot of questions! Unfortunately, he's been dead for about 1,500 years. I'm very grateful his words are with us forever…

Cultivate the inner self;
> **Its Power becomes real.**

Cultivate the home;
> **its Power becomes abundant.**

Cultivate the community;
> **Its Power becomes greater.**

Cultivate the organization:
> **Its Power becomes prolific.**

Cultivate the world;
> **Its Power becomes universal.**

Translated by R.L. Wing from The Tao of Power

PERSEVERANCE

I've got to tell you about my storied career as an amateur boxer. When people find out I was a fighter, they somehow assume I was good at it; I wasn't. To be fair, for a guy approaching middle-age and fighting full-contact big-boy boxing, I guess I was OK; but I knew going in I wasn't going to be a champion. I wanted to learn more about full-contact to further my understanding of fighting arts; and to be honest, I wanted to prove to myself that I could take it!

Anyway; my official amateur record is a remarkable 0-1. That's it! I had a few club fights and a few "unsanctioned" fights (details purposefully omitted!), but my official Boxing USA amateur record will forever remain zero wins, one loss.

My only recorded loss comes at the hand of a much younger, stronger and better fighter. The other middle aged guy I was supposed to fight scratched due to the flu. My trainer said there was a new fighter ready to take the fight; he seemed like a nice enough guy so I said "Let's get it on!" I also told my trainer that the other fighter's trainer looked awfully familiar. I wanted to know who these guys were; he said not to worry about it!

More important to the story is a group of loyal friends of mine sitting comfortably at ringside enjoying their beer and hot dogs. I'm sure my buddies came to see me launch the first in a series of mid-life crises adventures by dominating my first official boxing match.

What they saw that night was a young, strong, fast, and very skilled fighter; and that guy busted my nose and knocked me down in the first round. As I lay on the canvas, my only clear memories were how bright the lights looked from down there and the thundering voices of my buddies yelling, "Get up! Jim, GET UP!"

I somehow finished the first round; I can't remember how. I may not have been good, but I was either tough or stupid because I'm quite sure I finished the round in the fog of a full-on concussion. According to my trainer I sat in the corner, eyes open and unresponsive for a good 50 seconds, despite a bracing cup of ice he stuffed down the front of my trunks. Towel in; fight over.

There's a miraculous transformation that sometimes happens to a fighter once the towel is thrown and the bell rings. I thought I was ready to go! My trainer, thank goodness, thought it would be better to come back another night. My friends were still yelling for me to get in there!

Soon after, I figured out who the other guy's trainer was! It turns out I was fighting the son of Tony Lampron, the trainer of World Champion Joey Gamache. Tony was the guy I thought I recognized; here with his son, the alleged rookie! I don't think this was the kid's first time in the ring! Like me, I think his unofficial ring experience was deeper than his official record showed.

After the fight my friends took me out. It was my birthday and they thought a few adult beverages and gentlemanly entertainment would appropriately mark the occasion. In my concussion induced haze, I was in no condition to argue, so a quick shower and some first aid, consisting of stuffing a few balls of cotton up my broken nose, and off we went to celebrate at a venue dedicated to erotic dance artistry and elegant cocktails.

As I became a little more conscious and a little more inebriated I started to wax philosophically. I confronted my buddies, "Guys," I said, "I appreciate your support but if I'm laying there with my brains bashed out you guys should be yelling 'Stay down,' not 'Get up!'" They laughed; imagine that.

I will always remember that night; but what I told those guys was wrong! You do want people around you who are telling you to get up when you're knocked down. You want people in your corner who are telling you that you've got what it takes, even when you don't think so.

If people want to tell you what you can't do, get rid of them. I'm not saying you should surround yourself with ignorant "yes men" who won't give you an honest assessment, and I'm not saying you should be stupid; there are times when the wise move is to stay down. There are many more times when you've got to take the count deep, grab the ropes and climb back into the fight.

Here's the "fortune cookie" wisdom for this section:

"Knocked down seven times; get up eight!"

You could replace every book in your local library with self-help and personal development books and probably still leave out some titles. Just for fun I did a Google search for "personal development books" and got over 76 million results. That's probably a few more than your average library can fit on their shelves. Most of them are trying to find or reveal some "secret" to success and happiness.

I've done my share of research in this area. If you want to make substantive changes in your life it all boils down to one or two key components. Out of these the most consistent and important are:

- Discipline

- Perseverance

Big secret! Successful people work hard and they stick to it. Everyone fails, but something the average person doesn't realize is that the successful person fails more often than the average. You can guarantee mediocrity by inaction, but once you step in the ring, no matter how prepared you are, there's always a chance you'll lose. Don't let these knock downs and lesser set-backs turn into ultimate self-defeat. Train yourself to adopt a mindset of perseverance and you'll have what it takes to keep coming back after a loss. Cliché alert: You may lose some battles but you'll win the war!

Black Belt Mindset is about excellence, not mediocrity. Think Like a Black Belt and you're making a decision to get in the ring and stay there until you're punched out! If you let failures stop you, you better get used to being satisfied with whatever, whoever, and wherever you are right now. If you're willing to get up when it would feel way better to stay on the mat, then you have what it takes to excel. The rest is largely technical training!

Perseverance isn't limited to the mindset that you'll keep fighting as you're taking the blows. Perseverance is a close cousin to courage; it takes courage to keep going especially when the going is tough. Perseverance also covers those times when subtle dangers threaten your journey. It means you'll keep going when success is a distant spot on the horizon. In addition, perseverance is rejecting boredom as an excuse for anything and practicing a life of discipline and focus.

Like all the characteristics of Black Belt Mindset, perseverance is largely a decision. Granted, it's not always an easy decision. In fact, there are times when the decision to stay your course may not appear to be the best decision. Sometimes it might appear more rational or logical to change course or quit altogether to avoid catastrophe. There are other times when you're the only person who thinks staying on course is the wise decision.

If you've considered your options and you know in your mind and heart that the right decision is to press on, then by all means press on! "Damn the torpedoes, full speed ahead" can look stupid in the moment, but it may be exactly the right thing to do.

On the other hand, be careful not to press forward out of foolish pride or misplaced egotism. Perseverance can become a selfish obsession if you simply refuse to quit or redirect, even when your actions are obviously destructive, particularly when those actions affect others. The trouble is that it's sometimes hard to detect when perseverance crosses the line into stupidity. What keeps perseverance from becoming obsession is accountability. Know where you are and know what it's costing you to press an effort. Understand this cost in material, emotional and spiritual resources. For example, it's sometimes foolish to throw good money after bad. It's also foolish to destroy your marriage to save your business, and it's just plain stupid to throw away your health in pursuit of success. You might be able to make more money or find another spouse, but without health, there is no success! (I'm not joking about the money!)

Accountability is a discipline. You've got to find a way to track and monitor any worthwhile effort, develop a clear plan, and stick to it.

The plan helps you get back on course when you stray and gives you a road map to your success. Effective plans are well researched and documented. Put good information in and you'll have a reliable plan with predictable outcomes.

All good business plans have an exit strategy; a specifically defined point where the business will be sold, closed or transferred, and a specific course of action to do so when the time comes. Your life planning should encompass the same. Consider this: would you stick with an abusive spouse? Part of your life planning should be that you'll remain loyal and dedicated to a significant other until that person becomes abusive to you; then you'll leave. If you have that clear in your head before you make a commitment to a relationship, you're much more likely to persevere through life's mundane challenges.

Know what to do when times are tough, and when things are flush! The best business plans have some level of flexibility. Great business leaders also review the plan on a regular basis ready to make adjustments to changing conditions and circumstances, both good and bad. Too often prosperity leads to trouble when windfalls are wasted or spent frivolously without accountability. Part of any plan should provide for saving excess resources.

Emotional and spiritual resources can be "banked" away for a rainy day, just like money. The fact is, the more goodwill you extend into the world the greater your reserve of emotional and spiritual resources. This reserve takes form in the willingness of others to help you in times of need, or to simply offer encouragement and a pat on the back when you're down.

Perseverance depends on this reserve of resources. A constant commitment to personal development is essential in building these reserves. Learning new skills, acquiring new knowledge, and to paraphrase Stephen Covey, keeping your saw sharp will assure that you have the resources you need to persevere.

Surprisingly, you don't always need financial resources to persevere. It helps, but it's not necessary. Persevere, is what you do despite the fact that you're broke; however, you do need a reserve of emotional and spiritual resources. With emotional and spiritual reserves and some talent and ability, you can always find some way to produce material resources. The flip side is you might have all the material resources you can imagine, but without emotional and spiritual reserves you cannot enjoy success or happiness.

Here are the essential emotional and spiritual resources you need to sustain yourself:

- Knowledge

- Your skills, talents and abilities

- The goodwill or confidence of others

- Some degree of self-confidence

- Faith

Of all these resources, faith may be the most important. Again I'm not talking about religion, although for a lot of people that will serve nicely! I'm talking about some undying and relentless belief that there can be a positive outcome for your efforts. I'm talking about a core belief that you are a decent person and that you deserve to succeed.

I'm also talking about the fundamental expectation that life is worth living and that over time events in your life will generally work out for the best. This is the faith that says you'll probably be around tomorrow and it's prudent to take action to prepare for tomorrow.

Of course there are no guarantees; too many people wait for some sign of a guaranteed result before taking action. You don't need surety; in fact, if you were absolutely assured of a specific outcome, you wouldn't need faith. Faith is what keeps you driving your train through the tunnel long before you see the light at the other end. There is no perseverance without faith. Unfortunately, faith is becoming an increasingly rare commodity. We're bombarded with bad news 24 hours a day, 7 days a week. We're hooked on it! Like junkies we tie off and shoot our veins full of the stuff. This is a monkey you've got to get off your back! Why would anyone keep going today, knowing that within 10 years the whole world is going to be broke, sick, starving, or stupid?

Take a look at human history and you'll realize that some conditions are cyclical. A couple thousand years ago your world was collapsing if your village was wiped out by a band of renegades. Unfortunately, today the renegades can fly airplanes and launch missiles around the world. Our world is bigger than what we can see when we climb the nearest hill; our world includes neighbors we've never met and our actions affect people we may never see.

We live in a global society; therefore, what takes place on the other side of the planet does affect you. Stay informed; avoid being inundated. You can't focus on what you need to do if you don't turn off that noise once in a while, and believe me, this kind of noise can stifle your will.

To have the faith to persevere, you've got to stay focused on what you can do here and now. You've got to have faith that whatever you do will be important; it will contribute to your success and will bring value to others, as long as you're doing something positive.

We all have moments of doubt, particularly in the face of adversity, poverty or scarcity. When your perseverance is tested, take a break and do some accounting. Take an honest look at where you are now, review where you came from, and reassess your plan for the future.

You might find that you've already overcome some pretty severe challenges. That should renew your confidence and faith. If you can win once, you can win again! Even if you're dealing with poverty, scarcity, fear, or doubt; take an inventory of what you have materially, emotionally and spiritually. Keep in mind that as long as you're drawing breath you've got what it takes to move forward. If you're vertical and mobile, you're way ahead!

If you're experiencing authentic poverty in any key area, readjust your plan and prioritize any action that will help restore your reserves.

Then do it! There are no insignificant actions. The smallest step you take forward right now might in retrospect turn out to be the most important step in achieving your ultimate success.

Remember, perseverance is a decision. If you know it's right to stay the course don't allow yourself any but the briefest moments of doubt or inaction. Complacency is the most dangerous enemy of success. Keep moving and you've got a shot!

Too many people today are zombies. They go through life day after endless day moving without purpose. They keep moving but they don't know where they're going, where they've been, or where they are right now. They only know they're not happy. They're often pissed off at the world and ready to blame everyone else for their troubles. They're ready to surrender their freedom for the illusion of security, and they'll gladly give up the adventure of real life for a few relatively pain-free years of boredom.

Zombies don't practice perseverance; this is complacency. Zombies don't live; they survive. Don't be a zombie! Take the pain! "Take a bite out of the ass of life and drag it to you!"

Perseverance means staying on the journey, while dedicating yourself to your personal vision of success and happiness. You may have to change routes once in a while. You might have to stop and rest from time to time. You might have to winter for a while and re-supply before you continue the campaign. You may even have to "tactically re-deploy," re-fit and bring a new army to the field.

No matter what, just stay true to your ultimate vision and keep fighting. Knocked down seven times? Get up eight!

MASTERY

You might think this chapter belongs at the end of the book. Mastery is part of the process of perfection and it never ends. Mastery is the objective, but it's also the means. A true Master never feels a sense of completion, only satisfaction in the continual journey.

In a lot of martial arts traditions there were no formal recognitions of a "Master." The Master was the teacher; he was a Master because students sought his teaching. In traditions with a formal ranking system, sometimes the title of Master is degraded by politics or nepotism. Sounds a lot like business and real life, eh?

Authentic mastery is not the result of heredity or political position; it's not just the product of knowledge or even skill. Authentic mastery is a combination of talent, ability, proficiency, and perseverance. The bridge between basic skill and mastery is experience predicated on continual dedication to self-perfection; by now you should be noticing a consistent theme!

Mastery transcends skill and experience. Over time, if you develop your skills and talents to the best of your ability while maintaining a sense of wonder and humility, you may develop wisdom. Wisdom comes from experience forged by awareness or mindfulness over time. There are no shortcuts to wisdom and you can't proclaim yourself the wise man. Wisdom is not conferred; wisdom is recognized.

Excellence is consistently doing your best. Excellence leads to discipline and discipline over time leads to mastery. Mastery isn't just the result of all your hard work and commitment to excellence however, it's something beyond that. You know you've achieved mastery when other people express genuine respect for what you do, how you do it, and for who you've become through your work. Like I said, you really can't proclaim that you're a Master; other people recognize you as one when you're worthy of the distinction... and sometimes when you're not.

There are a lot of false masters in the world. Some are self-appointed; others have earned some degree of recognition, or sometimes by faking their credentials. A false master might also be someone who creates an exploitive sense of dependency among his followers. This is the line someone crosses when teaching is no longer about giving but taking. This is the problem with contemporary "gurus" who seem to have all the answers…for a price. Sometimes the price is only money; sometimes it's more.

An authentic Master does not make a living by selling secrets. Most of these so called secrets are painfully obvious truths. An authentic Master may make a living by teaching, coaching, consulting, or actually practicing his craft at the highest level. Teaching and coaching are drastically different than selling secrets. The Master's "secrets" are free; while the wisdom you receive is infinite and unconditional.

Believe it or not, there are days when my perfect martial arts students act like perfect little stinkers! On one such day I told my class that if they didn't start putting out some effort, I was going to cancel class. An emerging leader sounded off and said, "You can't do that! My Mom pays you for these lessons!"

"Oh ya?" was my articulate response. The young man and his classmates waited in stunned but anxious silence for me to blow my lid and finish whatever tirade was coming their way. Since I don't believe in blowing my lid in front of kids unless it's absolutely necessary, I just let the little anarchists stew in their own thoughts for a minute or so. Then I offered my explanation.

"Your Mom and Dad probably pay your tuition," I started, "That rents you a space on the floor, helps us keep the lights on, and helps your instructors to buy groceries once in a while. This is not, however, how you pay for your lessons. Does anyone know how you actually pay for your lessons?"

Without missing a beat, one of my young prodigies shot his hand up. "We pay for our lessons with respect!" That was it! Right on the proverbial nail's head! The Master is not paid in money for the secrets; he's paid by the respect of his students. That respect takes many forms, including the student's dedicated practice, attention and loyalty. The money pays for the room, or in the case of personal development, it probably pays for the books, seminars and DVDs you buy in your search for self improvement. When the Master starts to charge you for the secret, find another teacher!

An authentic Master that can show you how to apply the secret, coach you in the application, and guide you as you emerge as a Master, is worth his weight in whatever precious metal you care to apply to this metaphor!

So how do you become a "Master?"

In the first chapter I talked about action, and that the most important action is practice. Pick something to do and dedicate yourself to doing it as best you can for as long as it takes to become a Master. That's it; once again simple, not easy!

The secret to mastery is practice. I said I'd probably use this story more than once; it's a good one!

Remember Master Yamazaki's 3 rules for becoming a Master:

1. Basic practice.

2. Basic practice.

3. More basic practice.

Mastery isn't an end; it's a vocation. Mastery is a way of life and a mindset; Black Belt Mindset. Becoming a Master isn't the end of anything; it's the beginning of a life of sharing, teaching and mentoring. It's a dedication to becoming a living example for others. It's a life-long devotion to the continual process of perfection.

If you'd like to be recognized as an authentic Master you've got to accept the responsibility of teaching. That goes with the territory! Developing an extraordinary skill or talent and keeping it to yourself is the life of the hermit, not the life of the Master. Hiding your proverbial light under a bushel is not humility, that's just selfishness. When you become a Master you're going to teach. That's how you expand your effectiveness. That's how you create your legacy.

In a martial artist's life, the Master is a teacher. Think about some masters in business and personal life and you're going to find teachers there as well. Set your sites on becoming a Master and then teach others how to get there too.

The real power in your search for self-perfection is in helping other people take the trip as well. Imagine a society where the critical mass of people is all dedicated to self-improvement and sharing their experience with others. This isn't some kind of metaphysical exercise; I see this every day at Northern Chi Martial Arts Center. I see the power in this mindset in people from age three to grizzled old guys. This power transcends age, gender, and every other imaginable demographic.

Take a group of people and nourish their capacity for growth and self-perfection and you've got a dynamic and powerful group of people. Encourage them to teach others along the way and you've got a group whose impact will last for generations.

What would this mindset do for your organization or business?

Business power expands exponentially through teaching. The great teacher and pioneer of modern business training, John H. Patterson, once said, "Business is nothing but teaching." Teaching is really the sharing of power; teach well and the power of your organization multiplies. This truth should be self-evident; no one person can do everything, and as the power of a business expands, you need more people dedicated to each craft that makes the business strong.

Some people try to protect turf; they may be jealous or worried that someone is going to knock them off their perch. The fact is that if you're willing to develop your skills as a Master Instructor there will always be room for you at the top. You should be training someone to take your place; how else can you move up? A Master in business is always training his replacement so he can move on to bigger and better things.

Here's another in our continuing series of fortune cookies:

"The Master excels not by teaching his students to equal his abilities; the Master excels when his student's abilities exceed his own."

The Master is not looking to protect turf. He's looking to expand territory, and that can only be done by developing others with the skills and abilities to make his vision a reality. This is done by sharing, not by hoarding.

Rather than looking to ancient times for a good example, look at the story of Microsoft. Bill Gates built his empire by recruiting and training geniuses! His first generation of geniuses expanded their power by training successive generations. Instead of keeping the whole pie for himself, Gates shared the wealth and turned his geniuses into millionaires. The more they made, the more he made, until he became one of the wealthiest people on earth.

Contrast this with elite con-man Bernie Madoff. Madoff was looked at as a master; a guru in the world of investing. He kept secrets. He kept his most treasured secret for himself; how to rip people off on a scale nobody had previously imagined possible.

Who came out the better in the end?

Today we talk a lot about "brand." The brand of the Master is a valuable skill developed through dedicated training and experience, tempered by sincere humility and expanded through sharing.

Would you like people to associate "mastery" with your personal brand?

LEADERSHIP

What are the qualities of an effective leader?

Some years ago I started a Junior Leadership Team at my martial arts center. These are kids willing to dedicate themselves to helping other students by assisting the adult instructors and by serving as model students. Lead by example!

We hold regular meetings for these leaders-in-training. One session about 4 years ago laid the foundation for the form and conduct of our Junior Leaders from that point forward. I did a series of discussions with my advanced junior students to see how they would define leadership.

The three major qualities they came up with are:

- Courage

- Compassion

- Wisdom

Could you possibly improve on this list? From the mouths of babes!

If I'm remembering correctly, our little leadership conference ran about three weeks. Each day we'd commit about 20 minutes to this discussion. I wanted them to come up with the words; all I did was help out when we discovered a trait that these 7 to 12 year old students might not have the vocabulary to express. Even then, I offered them some options and the rest was up to them.

Wisdom started as knowledge. The first trait of an effective leader according to these emerging young leaders was that the leader had to know something; hopefully a little more than the people being led. I challenged them with this question, "Do all smart people make good leaders?" In other words, does the fact that you know a little more than the people around you make you a good leader?

The students said no and using the lingo of the dojo they said to be a leader, someone had to "walk the walk" as well as being able to "talk the talk." What they identified was that the most effective leaders have some degree of experience that transcends knowledge. The right word for this combination of experience and knowledge emerged as "wisdom."

People are more likely to follow a wise man than a wise guy!

Courage was put out there right from the start. Almost universally, the students said a leader must have courage. I've been leading these discussions for a number of years now and every group I work with seems to organically express courage as an essential trait of leadership.

All I do from there is make sure they understand that courage is not the absence of fear; you'll remember that the absence of fear is stupidity, not courage. Stupidity includes doing things that might look like courage, but only expose you to excessive risk without substantive benefit. Jumping your skateboard across a busy street on a dare is stupid, not courageous, whether you feel any fear or not.

Compassion took a little time to get to. I should mention that my students came up with lots of great leadership traits. I challenged them to reduce all these qualities to the three most important and inclusive.

The students said a leader had to care about his followers. I gave them a tough problem: What if you had to lead an army into battle knowing that you were committing many of your troops to death? What if you had to choose who would go into battle knowing the first wave is exposed to the most danger? These might be common enough problems for students at West Point, but our little leadership conference is often the first time these young people think about life on these terms.

The ability to make tough decisions involving great risk for the common good is really a product of compassion. Fortunately Samurai legend is full of stories of compassion for one's enemy as a process of self-perfection, so I was able to help the students focus several other traits under this word. They agreed that compassion included loyalty, caring, respect, and sharing.

We almost added respect and increased the traits of a leader to four. I asked whether leaders should command respect, or should they first offer respect freely? The consensus was that authentic leaders didn't need to "command" respect; respect was offered to them freely. Why? Because if you give respect without conditions, you're more likely to earn respect in return.

We're going to cover respect in this section in great detail when we talk about compassion. For now it's enough to say that my students felt that respect and compassion were pretty close cousins; after all, "Respect is the Rule of the School," so they'd already covered that!

What is very interesting is that any of these traits that involve some act of giving or submission on the part of followers is much more effective when that trait is first offered by the leader without conditions. To put it another way, compassion, respect, loyalty, and to some degree, wisdom should be first offered by the leader, unconditionally. This unconditional offering is much more likely to earn a return in kind.

Leadership is not a process of taking. It's a process of giving. Leadership is not the act of exploiting other people for your own ends. It's not the simple acquisition of title or station so you'll enjoy the associated privileges or benefits. Leadership is true sacrifice. A true leader is willing to sacrifice for the benefit of his followers.

One part of the discussion that didn't make that final cut, but always comes up, is that good leaders are usually good followers as well. This works a couple of ways. First, good leaders usually get that way by following other good leaders. Someone provides us with an example we want to emulate. Second, there are many times when a leader has to step aside and encourage dissent, invite counsel, and delegate authority. The most effective leader does these things without surrendering responsibility.

"Lead by example." Grandmaster Jhoon Rhee

Leadership is the ultimate expression of sharing. Please understand that I'm talking about leadership, not dictatorship. A leader earns his position by developing willing followers. The dictator subjects people to his will by force, violence, bribery, or coercion.

Everyone can, and should welcome the responsibility of leadership. This doesn't mean you have to captain a ship, run a major company, or get yourself elected to public office. Leadership should be an everyday commodity. Leadership should be widespread, not rare.

Some leaders are vocal, charismatic, and can command the attention of an audience. This type of leader makes a great teacher, executive, military commander, police or fire officer, or politician. A charismatic leader who is comfortable in front of people can inspire, motivate and excite others to action.

The other type of leader is quiet, often unnoticed. This type of leader simply does his best every day; he doesn't hide his excellence but neither does he put it on display. This type of leader inspires the guy working next to him on the assembly line, in the office or in the trenches. This type of leader can step up when necessary, but isn't looking for rewards and accolades.

The most dynamic leader is a combination of both. There are times when it is important to others that someone stand in the spotlight and act as a visible example. There are other times when the most effective leadership is simply taking the time to help someone else learn a skill, complete a task, or share a moment of encouragement.

The most effective leader can motivate an army or inspire extraordinary effort in an individual. Extraordinary leaders are comfortable sitting in front of a huge audience or meeting one on one. The leader, with Black Belt Mindset, understands how to adapt his leadership technique to the situation.

Most of all, the most effective leader is someone who understands that leadership is sharing, not taking. As a leader it's your job to share yourself with your followers. You share your knowledge, experience and wisdom. You share your strengths and when appropriate, your weaknesses as well. You share your empathy, sympathy and sensitivity, while maintaining an objectivity that allows you to make difficult decisions that may sacrifice short term gratification, security or safety, for long-term benefits or a righteous cause.

A leader may be an executive, a manager, officer, team captain, or president. A leader can also be a team mate, a co-worker, or a family member. Great leaders can be NFL coaches or Pop Warner coaches. A great leader can be President of the United States or president of the local Lion's Club.

I said that a leader is someone people follow willingly. There is a danger here; there are people who are very effective at gathering followers, but do not make good leaders. The other vital quality of a leader is one who can advance a cause for the benefit of the group. Be careful here too; you could make a reasonable argument that Adolf Hitler, even though he was a dictator, was for some, a highly effective leader. Leadership, like power, can be applied as easily to evil ends as to the common good.

People who gather followers, but have no substantive agenda, are not really leaders. They may be good entertainers or salespeople. The ability to entertain and to sell may be valuable skills for an effective leader, but these qualities do not define leadership. Be very cautious of the entertainer who never really delivers anything beyond the show, or the salesman who takes your money and runs.

When you decide to Think Like a Black Belt you're making the decision to be an authentic leader. If you're already considered a leader, you're making a commitment to improving your leadership skills, just as you made a commitment to continual self-improvement. Leadership is a means, not an end. Leadership is the means to a productive, happy and secure community, organization, team, family or nation.

Are leaders made or are they born?

Psychologists and philosophers have been debating this puzzle forever and they're no closer to a resolution today than in the days of Lao Tzu or Socrates. Some leaders do seem naturally born into the role. I'd argue that in most cases these guys didn't lick it from a rock. John F. Kennedy is quite often cited as an example of a natural born leader, but from his earliest years his father Joseph trained and groomed him to become a leader. He was given every opportunity to develop his leadership skills; to his credit, he took full advantage of these opportunities.

Other leaders seem to emerge from necessity out of extraordinary circumstances and conditions. Gandhi and Martin Luther King Jr. both professed to be reluctant leaders. Neither man sought the mantle of leadership, or certainly not the circus that goes along with it. Both these men talk about moments in their lives when they faced a moment of truth; would they stand up for what they thought was right or would they walk away and try to live ordinary lives? Neither man realized at the time what he might be getting into. Both accepted leadership roles that would ultimately shape and define their lives, in addition to changing the lives of millions of followers.

Leadership is often a choice. Each of us faces this choice from time to time. Sometimes walking away is the right decision. If your call to leadership doesn't match up to your skill set, you might have to pass; or dedicate yourself to a crash course in whatever skills you'll need!

One of my heroes, and an excellent example of true leadership, is Joshua Chamberlain. I live a couple of blocks from the house he occupied when he felt the call of leadership and left a very comfortable teaching post at Bowdoin College to petition for a commission in the Union Army. There is still a lot of political and historical debate about the root causes of the Civil War; Chamberlain had no such ambiguity. He felt compelled to serve the cause of preserving a United States and ending slavery.

Chamberlain was given a commission with the famous 20th Maine Regiment, heroes of Little Round Top at the Battle of Gettysburg. After returning home to let his wife in on his plans, Chamberlain set off to join the war. (Apparently these things were handled much differently in the 19th century!) The problem was that like many officers appointed politically, or by necessity, Chamberlain had absolutely no military experience. He was a professor of rhetoric and natural theology.

So, the only man in United States history to be promoted to general on the field of battle started his military career as an officer with no more knowledge or experience than a common draftee on the day he reports to camp. He was, however, a consummate student and a wonderful example of someone with Black Belt Mindset. He hit the books, literally, and trained with his Colonel Ambrose, a West Pointer, on the way to his first post. He would become one of the most effective and respected leaders in U.S. military history.

The reason Chamberlain is a hero of mine is his unwavering commitment to self-perfection. He saw the challenge and set to work to make himself worthy of the challenge. He integrated his skills and talents as a teacher with those of an effective military strategist; where he saw himself lacking he simply made the decision to improve.

Chamberlain also possessed another important quality of leadership: compassion. General Grant selected Chamberlain to accept the surrender of the Confederate Army and their materiel at Appomattox. He was chosen for this important duty because of his respect for his enemy and his attention to protocol. Most officers would have humiliated the surrendering troops and probably nothing would have been said. Chamberlain offered the surrendering army full military honors, and he and his men gave the defeated Confederates a formal salute. This gesture pissed off a lot of Union loyalists, but along with Grant's respectful treatment of General Lee, this thoughtful action began a process of reconciliation, which had a lot to do with healing the divided nation.

General George Patton defined leadership this way:

"A good general takes responsibility when things go bad and shares the credit when things go right."

Leadership, like all characteristics of Black Belt Mindset, starts with a decision. Are you willing to train? Are you willing to sacrifice? Are you willing to give your wisdom, compassion and courage unconditionally? Are you willing to put the needs of your followers ahead of your own? Are you willing to become the leader you'd be most willing to follow? Are you willing to lead by example?

COURAGE

Courage is not the absence of fear. The absence of fear is stupidity.

Courage is action in the face of fear. It's doing whatever it takes to get the job done, despite fear and doubt. Courage is about managing your fear and not allowing it to stop you, even if what you have to do seems stupid at the time!

There are three major types of courage:

- Heroic Courage

- Moral Courage

- Artistic Courage

Heroic courage is the most obvious and also the rarest type of courage. Many people believe this type of courage is rare because they don't imagine themselves capable of heroic actions. Think about the amazing story of Todd Beamer and the other passengers on Flight 93 during the 911 hijackings. These are the people who moved against the terrorists who had hijacked their flight after discovering the hijackers' plan to use their plane as a guided missile. When Beamer shouted "Let's roll" he wasn't giving orders to an elite counter-terrorist commando unit; he was leading a group of very ordinary people acting in the face of extra-ordinary circumstances.

Heroic courage is rare because most of us are not often exposed to the level of threat and danger that makes heroic courage necessary. This is just a small part of the reason to be grateful for law enforcement, fire service personnel, and our soldiers who expose themselves to this type of risk every time they punch the clock. In my experience, I've seen people act heroically who never thought themselves capable of such action. It does seem that at times, extraordinary conditions can bring out extraordinary courage.

Next is moral courage. Moral courage is the courage to do the right thing, even when the right thing is not popular, expedient, or profitable. Moral courage can be guided by one's religious faith, as an expression of respect, or as an obligation toward one's fellow man. In contemporary society, moral courage is becoming increasingly rare.

It's often easier to step on someone else's neck in life and business for personal gain. You might justify lesser acts of deception, subversion, or even violence in the name of greater gain. The truth is that most of the time the ends do not justify the means. Your life is a continuum of "the means;" the ends are fleeting at best.

Moral courage includes standing up for others who need your voice, support and help. It's also the courage to keep your mouth shut when appropriate.

The third and often most elusive type is artistic courage. You hear this expression used to describe someone who has created a change in art, music, dance, film, or writing. Everyone is capable of artistic courage, and every human expression has an artistic side.

Artistic courage is the ability to expose one's creativity to public scrutiny. It means honestly sharing your talents and abilities with the world without any guarantee that your expression will be accepted. Artistic courage is literally letting your light shine from under your bushel.

You may be a writer, a musician, or an artist. You might also have a new idea to improve customer service at your business. You might be a teacher trying a new way to reach your students, or a CEO who has an idea for motivating your employees. It might be that you're an ordinary person who has decided that you have a passion you want to share with the world; this is the courage of the entrepreneur.

Artistic courage is the most elusive because the process of creative artistry most directly exposes your inner self, and sometimes your most intimate or treasured thoughts and feelings. You're literally exposing your most vulnerable self to the scrutiny of others, and sometimes to the public; and there is absolutely no guarantee of success.

That's a scary place to be!

Courage is your ability to act in the face of fear and danger; however, fear is not usually our biggest problem. Trying to avoid fear is the real issue. Remember that failure is the result of fear, doubt and complacency. You can usually deal with fear and doubt somewhat clinically; complacency will get you killed every time! Ironically, complacency can really be a huge problem when you're trying to overcome fear and doubt. The strange truth is that you can become very comfortable with your fears and doubts and that's what makes the work of meaningful change so frightening.

One of the biggest problems in contemporary culture is that people will do almost anything to avoid fear, doubt and pain. The thing they do most is nothing. That's complacency, and that's a real problem! Change is often difficult and uncomfortable, but to move beyond your fears and doubts you've got to embrace change. You've got to leave the comfort of familiar fears and doubts and accept a little pain if you're going to make meaningful changes.

Your grandmother probably said this to you, but once again, good philosophy is always worth repeating; no matter what you fear it's always better to face your fears than run away from them. You can't hide from fear and doubt; complacency is death by a thousand cuts. Every time you run from fear and doubt a part of you is sliced away.

So what should you do when real fear and doubt show up?

"What do you do when you meet the devil on the road?"

Think about that for a few minutes. What is your natural reaction or first impulse when you're faced with something or someone you fear? What do you usually want to do when the outcome of your actions is uncertain, risky, or dangerous?

What should you do when you meet the devil on the road?

"Shake his hand!"

Quit or take action; only one of these choices guarantees a predictable outcome. You know what's going to happen when you quit: nothing! Choose action and all of a sudden you're throwing dice. Despite popular contemporary self-help mythology, action is no guarantee of success. The opposite is true; nearly any action is full of risk, and maybe the greatest risk is failure.

Failure might be your devil; shake his hand! Facing your fears is the first step, and I'd argue the only option, if you want to have some chance of success. Stepping on the field won't assure victory, but you can't do anything from the sidelines. Get in the game!

What do you fear? According to a fascinating study of top 10 fears complied by SelfHelpCollective.com , these were the top three results:

1. Fear of flying. (Or maybe fear of being stranded on the tarmac for a 4 hour flight delay with no water or peanuts!)

2. Speaking in public. (This fear sells a lot of public speaking courses!)

3. Fear of heights.

This data was produced by compiling the most searched for fear related terms on engines like Google.

For the record, fear of death comes in at number six, preceded by fear of intimacy! What the heck is going on here?

The Phobia Website has arachnophobia in first place, followed by "sociophobia," the fear of people or social situations. Death is number 10 on their poll! The world famous Gallop pollsters list the fear of snakes, public speaking and heights as 1, 2 and 3 and fear of death didn't even make their list!

OK, the fear of snakes and spiders is probably instinctive; let's cut ourselves some slack there. Fear of heights and flying might have some metaphorical connection to a fear of success and achievement, but that may be a stretch.

Here's the weird one: is it safe to assume that the average adult fears meeting and talking to other people and getting close to one another above the fear of one's own death?!

I really don't know if this is true, but it makes a great starting place for our discussion. I can believe these results are accurate, mostly because so many people are hesitant to face up to their real fears. That's why death shows up so low, or in the case of Gallop not at all. Who thinks about death every day? Probably old people and the terminally ill; that might be why they look more courageous than the rest of us when they're facing it.

Speaking in public and interacting with one another seem to be easy fears to mitigate. If you want to be less fearful about speaking in public, learn how to do it properly by practicing. If you fear intimacy or social interaction, you'd likely benefit by simply getting out a little more. There are very few fears that can't be conquered through practice; simple, not always easy.

Both of these fears reveal an important part of our mindset. Speaking your mind in front of others and interacting with people outside your comfort zone both expose you to danger. You might fail to make your point, you might be ridiculed or criticized, and you really might look stupid.

It makes sense to fear death, within reason. The fear of death is probably our most effective survival mechanism! The truth is, however, we all punched that ticket when we got on this train! You're not going to escape death, so it would be time well spent to contemplate the meaning of life and death once in a while.

Focus on life. It's important to appreciate each day of your life; there's that gratitude thing again, and make the most of it. Fear of death can prevent you from living and that's just a damn shame. Accepting death as an inevitable end causes you to appreciate life; that's a significant irony!

What is fear, really?

First of all, fear is a natural emotional response we have when we're exposed to danger. Fear is a blessing of nature. Imagine life with absolutely no fear; what would keep you from standing in loose rock near the edge of a cliff? Fear can keep anger in check or keep you from investing all your money in some scheme that seems too good to be true.

Fear is a blessing that reinforces your instinct for self-preservation; most of the time that's a good thing.

There are challenges, circumstances and conditions that warrant authentic, gut-wrenching, chest-tightening fear. Let's shake hands with a few of these devils:

- Loss of a loved one.

- Loss of a job.

- Loss of your home. (Seems loss plays a big role here!)

- Illness & serious injury.

- War.

- Authentic poverty.

- Violence.

- Natural disasters.

- Fire.

- Famine.

Most of these speak to circumstances and conditions outside your control. You may have done nothing to bring on these conditions, but even with the worst of them, you can still control your response and maybe even the outcome. It's understandable to fear these circumstances and conditions; most sane human beings would. Remember, courage is not the absence of fear. Courage will be your response to these challenges.

Heroes are born in the face of these legitimate fears. It's no small irony that when faced with serious conditions and circumstances many people act bravely; then deny that they had any other option! What else could you do? You can always lay back and let someone else fight your battle or wait for a savior. Courageous people act, they don't wait. When help comes, they appreciate it.

Here are some circumstances and conditions most people fear at one time or another. This is an entirely different level of fear. Look over this list and calmly ask yourself if any of these conditions should be paralyzing. They may have been in the past, but right here, right now you're just reading a book. These things can't hurt you right now.

- Failure.

- Doubt.

- Lack of talent or ability.

- Exposing your talents and abilities to open criticism.

- Poverty.

- Pain.

- Loss of esteem.

- Embarrassment.

- Lack of self-worth. (You can substitute "self-esteem" if you prefer.)

- Lack of meaningful relationships.

I'll skip all the traditional psycho-babble that usually softens the impact in self-help philosophy. The truth is, you can deal with every fear on this list. These are devils you can shake hands with, then throw the sucker over your hip and drop an elbow on his head!

Notice that in the first list you're dealing mostly with authentic loss. In the second list, the theme is scarcity more than loss. These are things you lack or never had, not things that have necessarily been taken away from you. Even if they have been taken away, with some courage, discipline, focus, and perseverance you can get them back.

Notice also that poverty is on both lists. I agonized over putting poverty on the second list; however, it is a fear than many of us face sometime in life, but one that can usually be overcome. Authentic poverty means something has happened to take away your ability or capacity to provide for yourself. Authentic poverty can be the result of a natural disaster, economic collapse, war, violence, famine, old age, injury, or illness. In some cases, you may be born into it. Small children do not have the capacity to change authentic poverty; yet.

Poverty on the second list is poverty you can change. I'm not saying you shouldn't be afraid of it; we're all legitimately frightened by the prospect of poverty from time to time, but you can do something about it. As long as you're drawing breath and you have your health, talents and abilities, you can effect change. Even if you're experiencing authentic poverty as a result of circumstances and conditions beyond your control, you may still have the ability to overcome it. For example, you might have lost your home and your savings because of a tornado, but as long as you escaped with your life and health you can rebuild. You may have been diagnosed with cancer and that may have drained your material resources; but if you're on the road to recovery, you once again have the opportunity to create a life of success and happiness.

To change circumstances and conditions you've got to take action. Every fear on that second list can be overcome through action. Take action and change the conditions on that first list and you're a hero.

Every one of us has fears and doubts. Some of these fears and doubts might look trivial to one person and might paralyze someone else. I'm not here to judge, and I wouldn't advise you wasting your time judging others either; that's not the solution. Courage means recognizing your fears, shaking hands with the devil, and taking action to change your circumstances and conditions.

Some years ago I attended a conference for people in the martial arts business. The seminar leader stood in front of a room full of Black Belts who made their living teaching martial arts. He got everyone's attention when he stepped up and said, "Everyone who earns a Black Belt starts out as either a wimp or a blimp!" You could have heard the proverbial pin drop.

His intention was to convey that every one of us had, at some point, faced one of two major challenges in life that martial arts training would help us overcome. Each of us had either started a martial arts program to get in shape, or to address some ominous personal development issue. A lot of people gravitate toward martial arts to work on deficiencies in self-esteem, confidence, and discipline. I can tell you this, he struck a nerve! I didn't know if he was going to make it out of that conference room alive!

Most of the professional martial artists in that room were offended. Why? There are a lot of people who come to martial arts with a well-developed sense of themselves; but I have to honestly say, the majority come with an agenda. Most people come to the martial arts to improve themselves. That's nothing to take offense to; in fact, it's something we should celebrate.

I admit openly that when I first decided to try martial arts, it was to get through one of the worst times in my life. I had NO self-esteem. I had no sense of self-worth or value, I and was extremely lacking in self-confidence. I did have a fairly good work ethic and a high tolerance for risk; but I have to honestly say that mostly came from a "what do I have to lose" attitude more than any sense of courage.

I was blessed with a well-developed sense of personal responsibility, so I wasn't blaming anyone else for where I was in life; I just figured I deserved what I got. At that point in my life I was a recovering drug abuser, my passion was music and my first successful band was breaking up, and my fiancé was leaving me for someone with a better sense of direction in life. She took the car and our brand new color set, during football season no less! I figured I got what I deserved; maybe I did!

It was at this point in my life that I somehow decided to shake hands with the devil. Why was I such a failure? Why did the woman I love leave me? Why was I broke? Was this just the way life was supposed to be or did I somehow create this mess by being some kind of asshole?

At my lowest point I had no material resources; no money, no property of any value, literally just the clothes on my back. I was holding down a job and thankfully the people I worked for were kind, understanding, and supportive. It would be years before I realized just how much so. Now I can recognize this support system as an abundant part of my emotional resource inventory. At that time, I felt nothing but poverty, materially, emotionally and spiritually. I was ready to toss the whole mess, lie down and quit. You can imagine for yourself just how far I would actually let myself go down this path; your worst imaginings would probably not equal what I was actually contemplating in that desperate moment.

This was one of the many moments in my life where I faced a clear choice: quit or do something. I chose to do something, and that something was to start martial art lessons. I had no idea what I was in for. Looking back, I can say that on that day I started to face my worst fears. I started to move beyond the lies I had been taught and believed about my self-perception and expectations for life. I started a life that would teach me how to embrace self-perfection, accept criticism as part of growing and failure as part of success.

At the time I just figured I would try the introductory program, and at worst, I'd have some cool souvenirs: a karate belt and a pair of pajamas!

It would be dishonest to say I had any great awakening at this time. I experienced no flash of enlightenment; I found out later that those moments are hard earned and fleeting. I can say that I knew pretty early on that I had found someplace where people were seriously dedicated to one thing and only one thing: making themselves better. Later, I'd discover that this process of self-perfection is the life of a Black Belt.

When we're having our "wimp or blimp" moments, why can't we just wake up and start making the changes that will make us feel better? Why during these moments does it seem that quitting, even sometimes just lying down and dying would be the best solution?

When we're facing fear there is really only one solution: COURAGE!

Courage, belief, and self-confidence are developed and earned; and you earn them by facing adversity. The good news is that courage is a quality accessible to anyone at any time. All it takes is a decision and an understanding of what courage really is. Remember…

"Courage is not the absence of fear. The absence of fear is stupidity!"

Too many people confuse the experience of fear with a lack of courage. The two are not mutually exclusive; in fact, you can't have one without the other. Courage isn't the absence of fear; it's the ability to do what you need to do when you're facing fear. Ironically, I've seen seemingly timid people act courageously in dangerous situations. I've also seen people who talk a good game and may seem outwardly courageous, that fold in the face of daily challenges.

Looking at my own life, and maybe you can identify with this, I tend to avoid facing some of the least difficult daily challenges to avoid minor aggravation, pain, and set-backs.

It seems that somehow most of us are wired to avoid risk. Even if in the long run the more difficult option is the best one, it's sometimes very difficult to get moving in the right direction. As bad as things might be, it's seems safer, or less painful, to stand still or quit.

That's why some people will stay with an abusive partner or spouse rather than risk being alone. It's why you'll placate the bully even though we know he'll be in your face again tomorrow. It's why you'll wait for the dreaded call instead of picking up the phone to negotiate with a bill collector. It's why mediocrity is sometimes a more comfortable companion than the risk of failure in the pursuit of excellence. This is why I took drugs instead of going to my college classes.

Sometimes, we'd rather stay with what we know than risk taking a chance on something different. Most of all, we're afraid of failure. That may sound stupid when I'm describing such desperate conditions, but when you already consider yourself a failure, it's safer not to expose yourself to another failure; even when the real failure is in doing nothing.

When I started, what was to become my life as a martial artist, everything I was afraid of was waiting for me in the dojo: self-doubt, fear, and complacency. That's how I was able to reduce these fears and simplify the process of failure into 3 manageable components:

- Fear

- Doubt

- Complacency

Fear and doubt are components you can work with. Over time, with motivation and discipline, you can learn to control fear and overcome doubt.

It takes courage to overcome fear, doubt and complacency because it seems that the human being is hard-wired to preserve the status quo even when present conditions are undesirable. The greatest fear many people have is the fear of the unknown, so even lousy conditions you're familiar with might be more comfortable than risking change.

And here's the rub: with any action, you expose yourself to risk. If you want to guarantee a predictable outcome, quit. When you quit, you know what's going to happen: nothing. As soon as you take action you're taking on risk. If you want to change, you've got to take a chance. If you want to succeed, you've got to risk failure. That's the price.

Once you develop a sense of courage, you can face your fears and doubts. You may not always win, but when you choose to fight, you're prepared to fight to the death. In the art of Kenpo this is the core philosophy of "Fighting Spirit," represented by the dragon. You'll certainly have plenty of opportunity to test your courage against the daily challenges of life and some of these may be extreme. Sometimes the most intense challenges to your courage can be subtle. The most intense challenge is when your honor is tested.

Honor is certainly a central theme in martial arts philosophy, yet sadly a lost theme in much of contemporary society.

I challenge my young martial arts students with some expectations that are not popular at times. I expect them to tell the truth whenever possible and when it's difficult. I expect them to stand up for someone who is being picked on. I expect them to walk away from stupidity. I expect them to face up to their fears. I expect them to be excellent in everything they do. I expect them to live the Rule of Respect.

I also expect them to make mistakes; and most of all, when they do make mistakes, I expect them to take full responsibility. During these discussions, we talk about why they should practice these expectations. The biggest challenge is when we're talking about respect; as with love and compassion, respect is something that must be given unconditionally. In other words, you give respect without any expectation of return; but most importantly, you give it before it's offered to you.

I'm as honest as I can be with these kids. In fact, I usually start these discussions by asking them, "Do you want me to be nice, or honest?" Kids usually pick honest; adults sometimes opt for nice! If there's no guarantee that you'll get respect back, why should we show it?

"Because it's the right thing to do!" That's it; and all the kids at my center learn this early. It's simple, but not easy. Getting to Black Belt is simple, not easy. Getting through life day by day is simple, not easy. You often do the tough things because they're simply the right things to do.

That's what honor is all about. It's about doing the right thing even when it's tough.

Let's shake hands with the devil and see if we can't scare him a little. There's actually a logical progression you can use to develop courage:

First identify your fear; find out specifically and rationally what's scaring you. Caution; this might not be the surface fear, there may be something underneath it. You may be afraid of making cold sales calls; underneath that the real fear is that someone will coldly reject you. You may be afraid of asking someone for a date; underneath you may fear that you won't measure up to his or her standards.

Second, once you identify your fear, prepare yourself. Positive self-talk is helpful, but even more important is to think about what will happen if you fail. Most of the time the actual consequences of failure are far outweighed by the benefits you'll enjoy if you're successful! Don't let the fear of a little pain keep you from the rewards that go along with a successful outcome.

Prepare yourself as best you can to create the successful or desired outcome. To say it bluntly; do your homework! Most people don't fail because they suck; they fail because they were lazy! If you give it your best shot, the worst that happens is you're better prepared for the next attempt. When you do everything you can to face a challenge you become more confident, even in failure.

Part of your preparation should be what you'll do if you don't succeed. Will you simply make another call? If your dream girl or guy shoots you down, will you collapse or will you spend some time with friends who appreciate you for the special person you are? Will you waste time beating yourself for your mistakes or will you rework your sales pitch armed with new knowledge and experience?

It's strange, but so many times when you're rejected you will, at some point, find out that had you been successful, that an apparent opportunity would have turned into a disaster!

Finally, weigh the fear you might have in the possibility of failing, against the fear of never making the attempt. You may be sweating the possible rejection of your next sales call, but what happens if you make no calls? Shouldn't the fear of not paying your mortgage be a more serious consideration than the fear of rejection?

The more you face your fears, the more courage you'll develop. The more you shake hands with the devils in your life, the easier it is to greet the next one with confidence.

Having said all of this, fear and anxiety can become a serious and debilitating medical condition. There is never shame in asking for help in this or any other area of your life. If you think you really have a genuine anxiety problem, find a qualified professional to help you.

Taking action to find help is in itself an act of courage! By asking for help you are in fact facing your fears!

Fear is natural. It's part of our intuitive self-defense system. Courage is part of our uniquely human experience that enriches us beyond other creatures. A lion acts out of instinct, not necessarily courage. A lion probably doesn't weigh the long-term consequences of what might appear as a courageous act.

You do.

When you act courageously in the face of your fears, you become a hero. When others see you continually face your fears and act with courage, you become a leader.

COMPASSION

Compassion is the selfless quality of concern for others. Without compassion, the leader becomes a dictator.

As a leader, power is your ability to act effectively to help others realize true success and happiness. The greatest leaders have always placed their concerns for the welfare of others in equal, if not superior priority, to their own benefit.

The dictator crosses the line to where his own benefits outweigh those of the people who trust and follow him. How do you keep your interests in check against the needs of the people who place their trust in you as a leader?

You need to fully embrace the values of gratitude and respect.

Gratitude is the empowering quality that may be the most important part of compassionate leadership.

Authentic leaders are grateful for the faith and trust others place in them. They are grateful for the knowledge, experience and wisdom they share. Authentic leaders realize that they could have, just as well, been born without the capacity to convert personal opportunity into power and leadership. They could have gone through life without the blessings of the challenges and adversities that reveal and test their capacity for leadership.

Gratitude is empowering when you appreciate that your leadership is the product of the faith and trust of your willing followers. You fully acknowledge that leadership power comes from the consent of those who follow you willingly, because without their consent, your power is lost. You can become grateful for the opportunity to lead, since leadership is the fullest expression of self-perfection and personal development.

The trust and faith of your followers are constant sources of inspiration, motivation and instigation for you to be and do your best.

It drives you toward continual self-improvement and excellence and can build the confidence and courage you need to push the envelope, while exploring new adventures on the frontier of personal development and excellence.

It's critically important to make a distinction between compassion and kindness. Compassion is not necessarily kindness; sometimes you've got to be cruel to be kind! If not cruel, there are times when to really express compassion you've got to do something that might have the appearance of indifference at one end of the scale and extreme violence at the other. Sometimes this is a matter of perspective, particularly when it comes to doing physical harm or even taking a life to protect others.

On the other hand, kindness can sometimes mask less than honorable intentions. Let's define compassion as genuine empathy and caring for others founded in a sincere desire to do good. In this sense, compassion transcends legality and popular opinion. We're back to doing what's right because it's the right thing to do; not always the most popular or best supported position.

"Never mistake my kindness for weakness, nor my silence for ignorance."

Quite a few years ago, a friend of mine paid me a tremendous compliment by giving me this wonderful quotation. He had noticed that in several business negotiations I was polite with adversaries, kind even when I was not shown kindness, and I kept my mouth shut when my ego would have preferred to shout out. I'll admit that at times I'd later have to do an hour on the heavy bag to unload my pent up emotion, and it's amazing that I didn't bite my tongue off at the root. Still, Mom taught me a little about prudence, and martial arts helped me realize that loud is not always strong, and that victory does not always go to the guy who throws the first punch.

Kindness can sometimes be confused for weakness or an expression of weakness.

Compassion is, by definition, an expression of strength, and you'll need great strength to express compassion in difficult situations. Sending troops to face death is not an act of kindness; when you order troops into battle to protect the lives of innocent people, it is an act of compassion.

A leader cannot always afford kindness. It's nice when you can be kind, but sometimes you've got to do what's difficult, in order to be compassionate for the greater good.

Let's look at a less lethal, but equally important expression of compassion.

If you're a business leader or manager, you're a teacher. In any capacity, when you have to teach or train others, there will be times when you've got to criticize. There are times when you have to impose disciplinary measures. There are also times when it's difficult, if not nearly impossible, to criticize, correct or discipline with kindness.

Sincere critique is an act of compassion; even when your expression has to be less than kind. How is anyone supposed to improve without sincere criticism? How does one know there's something wrong without receiving guidance?

You don't have to go out of your way to be a jerk, but if you're unwilling to correct someone because of some misguided sense of protocol, you're doing a disservice to that person and to the others who depend on their performance. It's sometimes difficult to criticize and call someone to task. You might be worried about hurting feelings or wondering if you'll lose that person's friendship, respect or loyalty. Most of the time, respect and loyalty are more at risk when the other guy thinks that you're too weak to offer honest criticism.

This is particularly true when you're talking with children. Whether you're a parent, teacher or coach, kids can smell weakness from around the corner. They don't want insincere praise or false admiration; they want you to be honest and they want you to provide guidance and leadership.

So do grownups!

Compassionate leadership requires incredible strength. It sometimes requires that you act alone or swim against the tide to do what's right. It often means losing some to save others; such as, ordering the death of those you love most. The general in the field faces this decision every day. In business the death may be more metaphorical, but no less painful. This leadership demands personal sacrifice for the benefit of your followers.

A great leader also has compassion for his enemies. First of all, the greatest test of one's compassion is to understand and feel something for an enemy, even when it's inevitable that you'll do battle. Compassion for the enemy checks you against ruthlessness and preserves mercy.

In regard to enemies, compassion can again be confused with weakness. It is not weak to feel compassion for an enemy; it's only weakness when that compassion prevents you from doing what needs to be done. That could mean fighting and defeating your enemy even if injury or death occurs. To a soldier, a law enforcement officer or someone defending himself against a violent attack, this might mean actually hurting, maiming or killing someone. In business it may mean that you defeat your competition as you take care of your business, family and employees.

Compassionate people don't like to destroy the dreams of others.

Respect allows you to express compassion without weakness. I just gave you an example of compassion as being strong enough to criticize someone for his own benefit, even when that criticism might not make you popular. If you refuse the responsibility to lead, correct when necessary, or make difficult decisions, you will lose the respect of your followers. To earn their respect, you've got to demonstrate respect for others...unconditionally.

Respect is defined as a means to hold something or someone in a position of esteem or value, or to act with deference to someone's position, station or role.

According to a seven year old boy I met a few years ago, respect means much more than this and it's much simpler to understand.

I was asked to give a talk on respect and responsibility at a local elementary school. I started my presentation the same way I do today; I asked the audience to give me a definition of the word respect. I was ready to take my time as 6 and 7 year old kids usually try to define the term using the term; they don't usually have the vocabulary to succinctly express such an intangible concept.

Boy was I wrong! A young man from the first grade stood up, bowed and said,

"Sensei, respect means taking care of one another!"

You may as well have kicked me in the stomach! I was speechless. I have to admit it took me a few seconds to compose myself. I sat down to catch my breath. Once I stood up and returned his bow, I told this young man that this was the best definition of the word respect I had ever heard.

From that moment on, I adopted this first grader's definition of respect for my work. In one short phrase this kid summed up everything important about respect. I sometimes shorten it to simply "taking care," but the bones are there. Respect is caring.

At the time I was teaching five basic rules for conduct in my martial arts centers:

- Effort

- Etiquette

- Sincerity

- Self-Control

- Character

As I thought about what this young man had just taught me, I realized that I only needed one rule: The Rule of Respect. There's nothing wrong with those five original rules; they are the time-honored values that have been passed down to martial artists since the golden age of the Shaolin fighting monks. It's just that the Rule of Respect sums up all the reasons to practice these five values and any number of others, in one simple guiding principle.

If, before you consider any action, you simply apply the Rule of Respect you will act correctly. All you've got to do is consider whether your action shows caring for yourself, your environment, or the people who will be impacted by your decision.

Be careful, just as the paper tiger might roar, but doesn't have the resources to act, the paper pacifist may hide behind the Rule of Respect as a way to mask cowardice. There are times when you're actions are going to do some harm to yourself or others, but if your actions are sincere, with the greater good in mind, you'll do the right thing even when it's difficult.

What would you do in this situation?

You're a cop responding to a domestic violence call with your partner. On the way you know that you're responding to the apartment of a disabled man with a long record of criminal violence.

You enter the apartment and see a man in a wheelchair bleeding badly from the abdomen. There's a woman in the room screaming; the man in the wheelchair is yelling that he's going to kill her. You see a knife in the man's hands, and you and your partner both draw your weapons and order him to drop the knife. Your partner enters the room to try and protect the woman when the man charges him in the wheelchair. You order him to stop; armed with the knife he continues to charge your partner who is now pinned in the corner of the room.

Do you shoot a guy in a wheelchair?

No reasonable person with a healthy mind wants to take another person's life. No matter how righteous you are in your actions, causing serious injury or killing another human being is not something most people want to consider; and there are always consequences to live with afterwards.

The story I just shared with you is not hypothetical. This was the real life scenario faced by two compassionate and dedicated officers. I know both of these men personally and I can assure you this was the last possible situation they could imagine or want to be in.

The second officer fired and saved the life of his partner. I was both honored and humbled when this officer called and asked if he could come and talk with me. He had done some training with me, but I felt compelled to start the conversation by saying that I recognized the blessing of being able to train and literally play at combat as a professional martial artist. I've never taken another person's life and I hope never to have that experience; I just wasn't sure what good my opinion would be to this man.

In the course of the conversation it was obvious that the officer knew he did the right thing. If he hadn't acted immediately, his partner would likely be dead. As it turns out, the shots the officer fired were not the cause of the assailant's death; his own self-inflicted knife wounds were ruled the cause. If he had dropped his weapon and surrendered; there would have been no way to save his life.

The officer knew he did the right thing. He didn't feel guilt, but he did feel a deep sense of regret. Unlike many of his fellow officers who had served and taken lives in military combat, my friend entered the force from civilian life. He was comfortable with the outcome, but couldn't help wishing it had turned out differently.

All I could do was thank him for sharing his story with me. This was a unique look into the consequences of taking a life in the most justified circumstances. I had to say that I didn't think it was inappropriate not to feel guilty. In my heart regret was the appropriate emotion; there was no reason to feel guilt.

The press didn't seem to agree. The news media highlighted the aspect of the assailant being restricted to a wheelchair. The inevitable question that circulated throughout our community was how could the cops gun down a guy in a wheelchair? Couldn't they have subdued him without shooting him?

Most people are compassionate; it's understandable that they'd weigh the wheelchair into the equation and look for some more humane solution to this situation. Of course, most people have never faced a violent attacker in a small space with blood flying, screaming and the imminent threat of death to a colleague staring them in the face. Would it have been more compassionate to try and stop the attack by another method? Would the officer be judged as compassionate if his partner was killed?

This is exactly the kind of decision a leader faces every day; sometimes literally and sometimes metaphorically. Sometimes your actions are going to cause collateral damage. Sometimes the greater act of compassion is to act decisively to prevent greater harm. A leader has to prepare himself to live with the consequences.

The Rule of Respect should not prevent you from taking action when necessary. It simply allows you to give full consideration to the consequences of that action. Sometimes you've got to act instantly with whatever information you have; and other times you've got to depend on instinct.

The more you train and prepare yourself, the better able you are to act quickly and correctly in difficult situations. This training is as important in business and personal life as it is in self-defense, maybe even more important.

You may never face a life and death encounter, I sincerely hope you don't; but you will be faced with decisions in life and business that affect your life and the lives of those around you. Living the Rule of Respect requires constant training and self-perfection.

In leadership, compassion is about placing the greater benefit of others above your own self-interests. It's about recognizing the needs and sometimes the suffering of your followers whether you directly feel their pain or not. Compassion is about making difficult decisions for the greater good, even when your decision might make you unpopular.

Some people genuinely abhor violence or bloodshed in any form. Gandhi was a courageous man; while he lived a life of non-violence he often put himself in harm's way to further his cause.

On the other hand, those who do the dirty work shouldn't be judged out of hand, or out of ignorance. Imagine the world without the men whose courage and foresight understood the real threat posed by Hitler and took action to stop him. It's true that violence always begets violence, but appeasement can cause even greater harm.

Compassion is not always an act of kindness; it's sometimes an act of great courage.

An effective leader has the ability and wisdom to express great kindness whenever possible, and has the strength to act decisively when necessary for the good of his followers no matter what the personal cost. That's true compassion.

"It's better not to fight.

"When one must fight it's better to injure than maim;

"It's better to maim than kill

"For all life is precious and can never be replaced."

-Ancient martial arts saying

WISDOM:
THE BEGINNER'S MIND

Knowledge is not wisdom. Wisdom is knowledge expanded by experience. Wisdom is the product of knowledge, learning, courage, perseverance, reflection, adaptation, and self-perfection with equal parts of blood, sweat and tears to season the experience.

Lots of inexperienced people possess a lot of knowledge. In our age of hyper-specialization, you can find high school kids gifted intellectually in any number of specific areas, such as, art, music, science, or math.

Wisdom transcends knowledge. Sincere reflection and introspection are essential if you want to develop authentic wisdom. Live, and experience life through the dynamic component of time; then let it all simmer in the pot of self-reflection and you might become a valuable sage. We need the sage to move the human species forward.

To truly be a wise person, you've got to understand Beginner's Mind.

Beginner's Mind is the mind of the Master, not the novice; it implies an awareness and understanding of the process of preserving the sense of wonder and curiosity that drives continual personal development.

When you start any adventure, you definitely think like a beginner. You're full of curiosity, excitement and energy. You haven't been at it long enough to be bored, jaded, skeptical, or completely exhausted. You also don't have the experience or perspective to really appreciate Beginner's Mind; it's all you know. You're like a fish in water; does a fish know it's in water unless you toss him up on dry land? Without something to compare it to, Beginner's Mind is difficult to understand.

Dedicate yourself to the perfection of any skill, trade, or profession and you'll inevitably experience periods of doubt, skepticism, pain, boredom, and fatigue. If you suffer long enough and really stick with it, you'll get to a level of mastery. If you can also learn to preserve the same feelings you had when you started, you'll always find some new challenge, adventure or opportunity no matter how far you've gone in your journey. When you can control your access to these feelings, you've achieved Beginner's Mind.

Beginner's Mind is a state of humility. It's also the process of cultivating curiosity, a sense of wonder in all things, and embracing the never-ending process of self-perfection. In the culture of the martial arts, those who have a profound understanding of these principles are called "Masters."

The great Asian philosophies are deeply embedded in modern martial arts culture. These philosophies look at life as a cyclical, rather than a linear experience. You start any new adventure from the perspective of a beginner; keeping beginner's mind is really the key to developing mastery. The Master knows that only a healthy sense of curiosity, wonder and gratitude gives you access to the deepest levels of wisdom and training in any discipline. Curiosity, wonder, and your desire to continually perfect yourself, provide the energy that sustains your practice long enough to become a Master.

Face it; people who become bored are boring! People who think they're great, are great; at least in their own minds, and that's as far as they're likely to take it. If you're bored or great (in your own mind) you've probably reached the highest level possible in your endeavor; at least until you change your mindset and adopt the mindset of the beginner.

When I earned my first Black Belt, my Master gave me a special gift. He gave me a heavy-duty Black Belt to wear in place of the economical version presented to me at my ceremony. He told me that if I continued my life as a martial artist, I'd probably tie and untie my belt thousands of times. He said that after a while, the rich, dark color would fade and my belt would become worn and frayed.

I knew what he was talking about. His was a bit worn and the Master above him, Professor Nick Cerio, had a belt that was so frayed it almost came apart at the knot. When you looked at the Professor's belt, you knew this guy was the real deal. The only way to put that much wear on a belt was to put mileage on the wearer! I remember one time when someone joked with the Professor; "When are you going to get a new belt?" My best recollection is that the Professor fired back something to the effect, "Never! You put me in the box with this belt."

The significance of the frayed belt runs a little deeper than the wisdom implied in the weathering. Brand new, your Black Belt is a rich, deep tone of black. This is just the outer covering. As the belt wears this black covering starts to slowly peel away. Under that black cover is an inner core; a belt of a different color: white.

The white belt represents the beginning of the whole journey as a martial artist. The white belt is the first belt you're given, just enough to keep your uniform jacket closed during training. Every time the seasoned Master ties on this beaten and worn Black Belt, he should be reminded of the continual cycle of martial arts life, and of real life too! Every time I tie on my belt, I'm reminded to keep beginner's mind, to approach every new day with curiosity and wonder and a commitment to continual self-perfection. What a truly beautiful symbol!

Earlier I told you about the first time I entered a "dojo." It was one of the lowest times in my life. My fiancé had recently left me for someone she rightfully believed had more ambition and prospects: a professional hockey player. At the time, I was a musician and my band had just split, as all bands eventually do. I had no car, no money, and I was living in a small apartment equipped with a few pieces of cheap department store furniture, a 10 inch black & white television set, and some milk crates.

I had a decent job at the time; I was working at a television station as a producer for TV commercials. I should have been able to hold on to a little money, but my music career and associated zeal for partying kept my financial portfolio at a level far below the poverty line. I have to be honest; I've got absolutely no idea where any of my money went.

By any measure, I was a failure; at least that's the way I looked at it. When I did have success, I lacked the sense of self-belief and confidence to recognize it as anything but an accident. I still needed to learn that success is seldom, if ever an accident, and that you'd better recognize the talent and abilities that bring you a success if you want to realize any of your dreams. A lack of self-belief and self-worth only leads to depression, failure, and an endless series of payments on a credit card reserved for bar tabs.

It was at that time when I walked into a dojo for the first time. I credit my brother, who had been pestering me for a couple of years about the benefits of martial arts. According to him, martial arts would be the answer to my problems. In the dojo I'd find self-confidence, belief in myself, and what I would later come to define as power.

I really didn't believe him. One day I was feeling really low and just had to get out of my crummy little apartment. I took a walk. I happened to look up at the side of a building and saw a 20 foot sign with gigantic letters that spelled out the word "K-A-R-A-T-E."

You could reasonably assume that at this point, my life would be changed forever. I've been a martial artist for nearly 25 years, and a professional for about 20 of those years. In that time, I've founded my own martial arts system, earned a Master's ranking for my work with cane fighting, I've been featured in Inside Kung Fu magazine twice, and was inducted into the US Martial Arts Hall of Fame as Master Instructor of the Year.

However, on the day I first walked into a dojo, you wouldn't have assumed that I'd become a professional martial artist any more than I did. I didn't even think I'd ever become a Black Belt; I certainly had no idea how to think like one, never mind how to act like one. I had no idea what it would take to become a Black Belt, nor any clue as to the tremendous impact martial arts would make on my life.

Here's what happened: I walked up a flight of stairs to the second floor dojo, watched a couple of guys throw each other around, and thought about how cool it would be to do that...

...then I turned around and walked back down the stairs. To this day I'm grateful that Dick Roy Sensei needed students and chased me down the stairs and talked me into enrolling in his beginner's program.

To a beginner, the symbol of success in martial arts is the Black Belt. I took a little longer than the average student to get there. My trip was interrupted by my personal struggles with self-doubt, a crippling lack of self-worth, an absence of self-confidence, and an almost never-ending propensity toward self-destructive behavior. It's not that I was a bad guy; had you met me then you probably would've thought I was a pretty nice guy, maybe even interesting, intelligent, and engaging. The problem was that I hadn't learned to recognize those qualities in myself. To me, every failure just validated that I was getting what I deserved: nothing. Any success was just a lucky scratch on a lottery ticket with a small prize that wouldn't last long. In fact, I was just like the guy who wins a $10 scratch ticket at the local convenience store, then turns around and buys a case of beer and another ticket with the winnings.

You know by now Black Belt Mindset isn't about becoming a millionaire, it's not about "get rich quick,", and it's not about the "secret" solution to all your problems. It's about finding success the hard way, the only way that's real and lasting. I told you how I earned my Black Belt in martial arts and how I learned to take the same process and apply it to life outside the dojo. Black Belt Mindset is about how you can utilize this same process to create your personal vision of success and happiness.

If I had to give you a specific definition of success and happiness for your life, I'd have to pass. I don't know what it's going to take to make you feel successful and ultimately what's going to make you happy. To be blunt, that's your problem!

It's also your blessing. It's up to each of us to define our own personal vision of success and happiness. If you're reading this, it's likely that you live in a country or society that allows you the opportunity to pursue these goals. If not, you're at least aware that such places exist and such opportunities are available to you. The ultimate expression of freedom is freely choosing what you're going to do with your own life. You're free to choose exactly what it takes to make you happy, and therefore successful.

Success and happiness are very personal issues. One person might not feel successful until he makes his first million. The next guy might be happy making $35,000 a year living in a mobile home and spending his spare time stocking his freezer with fresh venison. I was successful when I was just scraping by living in my small apartment and playing music; I didn't understand how to recognize or appreciate my success at the time.

In my past lives, I thought successful people were those guys who had yachts docked in the marinas in Portland harbor. I thought success meant having a chick-magnet car, a lot of money, and a fabulous looking girlfriend. I thought success was being famous and having a hit record, (CD's were still pretty new then and we actually still played vinyl records!)

In keeping with the theme of this book, I can tell you I finally learned about success by earning my Black Belt. That would make a nice story, but it's not true. It was a long time after I earned my Black Belt that I really started to understand the components of success, but it was a start!

My problem, and this is a problem shared by many other people, was that I kept measuring success by comparing myself to others. I saw success as the end instead of the next beginning. When I learned about Beginner's Mind, I started to enjoy success in smaller chunks. Ironically, I started to see a small success as part of the next adventure. I could see each failure as part of the next success.

Earning a Black Belt is certainly a success, but it's a beginning, not an end. The cool thing is that with each new beginning you're better equipped to enjoy even greater success, as long as you allow yourself to appreciate what you've earned and what you can still learn. I tell my students that earning a Black Belt, is like learning how to read; after you earn your Black Belt you can start learning how to write!

That's Beginner's Mind; an appreciation of the wonder and new-ness of each experience, opportunity, or disaster! It's an attitude of yearning, a kind of positive dissatisfaction with the status quo. You appreciate where you are, but you know there is always a new adven-ture coming your way. In a sense, each new beginning is a success especially as you become a Master! With each new exploit, you're operating on an elevated plane. You're moving in four dimensions and you're bringing new skills, talents, abilities, and wisdom to new levels. Just be sure to bring the wonder and energy of the beginner.

The best way to keep Beginner's Mind is to always be a beginner... at something! You can learn a new skill or trade, learn to paint, play a piano, or dance; you can start a new career or train yourself for ad-vancement in your current occupation. Or, you can teach!

An effective teacher is completely immersed in Beginner's Mind. When you teach, you're in a constant process of helping others open their hearts and minds to new experiences. With each new student, you're reliving the process of learning that expands your mind with new perspectives and renews your heart with the joy of discovery.

There are two reasons I wanted to share the concept of Beginner's Mind in this section on leadership. As I already said, Beginner's Mind is really a quality of the Master. A Master who doesn't accept the re-sponsibility of leadership on some level is wasting his blessings and discrediting his teachers.

Secondly, the most effective leaders are always effective teachers, and the most effective teachers are perpetual students. The most effective leaders are people who never lose their sense of wonder and their drive to make themselves better. Whether they're born with a natural gift of charisma or not, the person who is driven to make himself better provides a magnetic example for the rest of us. Unless you've become jaded, you're much more likely to follow the guy who walks the walk.

Teaching is an important part of leadership whether you're talking about military leadership, politics, business, or family life. Patton valued his ability to train troops as one of his most important assets. The most important job of a parent, besides providing food and shelter, is to teach young people how to be responsible members of a community.

Teaching is so important to leadership because there is no greater expression of respect, caring and selflessness. When you teach sincerely, you're sharing your "self." It's not just knowledge that you share; it's the experience, wisdom, joy, and pain that makes you who you are. Unless you're willing to share yourself unconditionally, don't teach. You certainly won't lead, at least not for long.

Remove the sense of wonder that distinguishes Beginner's Mind, and you're not teaching; you're just lecturing. There is a huge difference. Teaching demands that you fight on the same mat as your students. You've got to allow yourself the empathy to feel what your students are feeling throughout the process of learning. You've got to be willing to stand next to your student and show them how it's done, either by doing it yourself or by mindful correction, and questioning that leads the student to the solution. This can't be done from a distance.

This works at home, at work, at West Point, or at the CEO's Club.

Most of all, Beginner's Mind distinguishes authentic passion from punditry. In any given field there are plenty of people who have knowledge and useful experiences to share. A leader emerges when one shines with the joy and wonder of continual adventure and exploration. Find a way to share your passion with authenticity and genuine enthusiasm and you will attract followers. Now you're building a team!

One of the most common criticisms of "the man" at the top is that he's forgotten where he's come from. He's "lost touch" with the needs of the man on the front line. She's "forgotten what it's like to be a teen." Keep Beginner's Mind and you'll never lose touch, no matter how far you progress.

Any point in the process of self-perfection is the first chapter in your next adventure. Keep that thought in your heart and you'll always have the mind of the beginner. Combine Beginner's Mind with your ever expanding inventory of knowledge and experience, and you've got authentic wisdom.

We're in an age that needs genuine leaders at all levels of business and society. We need leaders who help the guy next to him learn a trade. We need leaders to teach children how to solve problems in a world of perpetual change. We need leaders to restore ethics to business culture and protect the tremendous freedom available through entrepreneurship.

Like everything else in Black Belt Mindset, the process of becoming an effective leader is simple; it's just not easy!

1. Learn as much as you can, experience as much as you can, and commit yourself fully to the process of self-perfection.

2. Share your love, knowledge and wisdom unconditionally.

3. Keep Beginner's Mind.

4. Repeat.

Humility is a close cousin of Beginner's Mind. It might be better to say that humility is the product of Beginner's Mind. The air of quiet, unassuming confidence associated with martial artists is what most people would probably call "humility." Expressing humility as an active process, the process of continual engagement in Beginner's Mind assures that humility will never be a static condition. This kind of humility is a powerful moving force in the life of someone who is dedicated to self-perfection and excellence for the highest purpose of sharing and elevating others.

At every Black Belt promotion, I share a powerful bit of wisdom I found a long time ago. I can't remember who said this, but I do know it came from an Asian sage. If you're considering a tattoo, you could do worse than brand this someplace where you can see it from time to time:

"Before I was enlightened I carried my water and gathered my rice. Now that I'm enlightened; I carry my water and gather my rice."

That's Black Belt Mindset.

IT'S YOUR BLACK BELT, STRAP IT ON!

Wat's the pay-off? Ultimately, I suppose there needs to be some reason to Think Like a Black Belt. In our results driven culture, there aren't too many people who will do the work without some reasonable expectation of results. I suppose that's part of our nature; we want to feel some sense of progress and growth.

I can't tell you that Black Belt Mindset is the key to your success. I can't tell you that even if you sincerely integrate the philosophy I'm teaching here that you'll enjoy wealth, fame, or happiness. I can't tell you that you'll achieve all your goals, or that your hard work and passion will always produce desired results.

If anyone is telling you this crap, that's what it is: bullshit.

The plain fact is that there aren't any guarantees. When you embrace a life of self-perfection, you're going "all-in," all the chips are on the table. You're risking everything because you're risking your "self." You risk failure, you risk looking like an idiot, you risk being wrong.

Black Belt Mindset doesn't guarantee victory; it's how you prepare yourself to step into the ring...every day. The more disciplined you are with these concepts, the more power and control you have over your thoughts and actions. The more you control your own thoughts and actions the greater possibility you have for success; the more control you have over your life.

Don't expect guarantees; expect to be prepared to compete. When did competition become a filthy word? When did we start wanting security over the freedom to prove we're the best? Competition is a powerful and liberating force. Have we become so cowardly, so insecure that we fear getting in the ring and bloodying our noses? If you really fear getting hurt or losing, I can respect that. That's something you can change.

Some cowards hide behind the false fear that competition will destroy us all. Again I say bullshit.

Fair competition does not destroy; it makes both combatants stronger. Lack of competition makes you weak. Competition is the mother's milk of all human progress and innovation. We've bred too many weaklings in our society and become too comfortable and complacent.

Complacent societies don't progress; they stagnate. These societies are like over-protective mothers who make their kids wear hockey helmets to the playground. Kids who are never allowed to bump their heads aren't safe; they're crippled! Instead of learning how to watch out for things that will smash their heads, they become afraid of doing anything without a helmet! Complacent societies don't produce anything useful or interesting so they start to borrow. They borrow culture, art, and even technology. They become indebted and dependent on lenders, loan sharks, and thieves. The interest gets higher and higher until there's no way to get out of debt.

Complacent societies breed entitled citizens. Sound familiar? It starts with the best intentions; let's make sure everyone has the bare minimum. The problem is that as soon as we impose a baseline, any baseline, we surrender individual freedom and condemn ourselves to the worst fate of all: mediocrity. American society wasn't built to guarantee the bare minimum; it was built to allow the individual to freely express his fullest potential. Granted, the founders left some people out of this formula; that's a matter of context. They also left us the capacity to correct those errors and we've been doing that ever since.

American society wasn't built to make sure everyone would win; it was built to make sure everyone could play the game. Our job is to make sure everyone gets to play by the same rules and to make sure the ref isn't on the take!

Competition makes you stronger, and makes your opponent stronger. Your skills are measured by the strength of your enemy. The key to success is to always step up to a stronger opponent. You can only become champ by fighting top ranked opponents. You can only stay on top by defending your title against the top ranked contenders.

As I said, fair competition does not destroy. Here's a fortune cookie:

"The quality of the warrior is measured by the strength of his enemy."

If you're going to grow, you've got to test yourself; and at the same time you're helping your opponent. If you're not giving it your best shot, what test does your opponent have? How does he grow and develop?

The key to fair competition is respect.

Remember that first grader's definition: "Take care of one another." Become "one with your enemy." Compete, and at the same time find ways to cooperate. Can you share your innovation and advances? Can you leverage both your strengths against a common enemy?

Imagine a world where everyone is competing fairly in business, technology, and learning. Everyone can become stronger, innovative, creative, and passionate individuals.

Now imagine this world constantly creating respectful alliances against the next common enemy; not destructively, but progressively. Eventually we start to attack the common enemies that we all must fight: hunger, disease and injustice. Together we explore new frontiers and open up new territories in space, in the mind, and in the future.

But wouldn't it be easier if we just all got along?

No. We're not wired that way. True happiness doesn't come from complacency and passivity. Our nature is to grow, learn, explore, and compete. Competition elevates everyone; that is, everyone who wants to get in the ring. Without competition there is only entitlement; entitlement produces generations of people waiting for others to solve problems and provide comfort.

Ultimately, entitlement is really a way to avoid pain; but it fails miserably in that regard. Entitlement only adjusts the pain threshold to a manageable level.

Competition is painful. You take your lumps to increase your pain threshold. You also come to an intimate understanding of what real pain feels like. If you're a disciplined and compassionate person, this should make you more empathetic to those who experience authentic pain through no fault of their own. Authentic pain is suffered from genuine poverty, natural disaster, illness, tyranny, and injustice.

Help others out of genuine compassion, not out of fear; too many people exploit false compassion to control others. We just can't eliminate pain and suffering; it's impossible. We can't solve every problem; or at least we've got to accept that every problem we solve will be replaced by another.

What we can do is prepare ourselves for the battle. We can discipline and train ourselves to compete fairly by fully embracing the process of self-perfection. We can train others to compete on the same field.

Imagine a society where nobody is waiting for saviors, solutions, government handouts, bailouts, or entitlements. Imagine every individual working toward constant self-improvement. Imagine each of us bringing ever more value and worth to the world by sharing and exchanging that value with one another.

Maybe that's what going with the flow really means! Maybe the flow is toward progress, improvement and self-perfection; not stagnation. After all, going with the flow means we know how to work with the current, rather than against it whenever possible.

So who is the enemy? Who is it you're competing against? Your external opponents are obvious, but here's another fortune cookie for you:

"Your most formidable enemy is brushing his teeth in your bathroom mirror!"

To realize our full potential, focus on improving a little every single day. Honestly, we all want to produce results. Sometimes the only result you're going to produce is to improve yourself a little bit. Other days you're moving at light speed toward your goals. Black Belt Mindset gives you the foundation for facing this daily competition internally and externally.

The trick is not to be too attached to the results. Goals are necessary and important; Master Jhoon Rhee says, "The source of all human energy is a goal." Good advice, but make sure you're focused on the present moment; this is where you're making it all happen.

Goals put the "fu" in "kung fu!" I talked about motivation and discipline applied over time as the components of the Kung Fu Triangle. That's how you generate power and ultimately produce the results you want.

The words "kung fu" translated, literally means, "achievement through effort." The most practical translation I've ever heard for kung fu is "work." It's work that produces the highest levels of achievement and accomplishment, or mastery. The term "kung" is what translates most directly to work or effort; so what's the "fu?"

Your "fu" is entirely up to you! I won't impose my concept of personal success on you or anyone else; that's not my job. I have, however, learned that success does have some common characteristics no matter who you are.

Success is a general feeling of abundance. To a certain degree, it's a sense of security, not necessarily in tangible evidence, but in your ability or capacity to do what it takes to produce this abundance. It's also about the faith you have in your talents and abilities in developing the courage to get you through the tough times. Success is simply having enough.

To feel successful, you need enough in 3 key areas of life: material, emotional and spiritual. How much enough? That is entirely up to you. I've learned that my sense of enough has evolved over time. My sense of enough in material life has certainly changed a lot since I've recognized that I have nobody but myself to depend on to provide for my security when I choose to retire. It's funny how your perspective changes when you're lucky enough to survive to middle age!

When you have enough material, emotional and spiritual resources at any given time, you should experience a feeling of success, as long as you've learned how to recognize the abundance you enjoy. Much of the trick is to realize when you have enough. The "secret" to recognizing abundance and success is gratitude.

Our collective inability to appreciate the resources we have all around us has crippled our society. I don't need research to back up this statement. I've lived it. I spent much of my life, same as most people, worrying about what I didn't have rather than appreciating what I did have. I complained about my jobs, bitched about "working for the man," and sang in harmony with a lot of others of my generation who pitched a fit of discontent with the system, while maintaining a comfortable distance from the burden of participation. We waited for someone to do something about our condition. That wasn't only a mistake; it was wrong.

There are people in the world who face the daily threat of institutionalized starvation, rape, murder, and genocide. While there is still legitimate poverty in America, the vast majority of people in the United States that face hardship have people to help and systems to rescue them. In most states it's against the law to turn anyone away from a hospital emergency room, regardless of their ability to pay for treatment. Some reports indicate that 85% or more of Americans below the poverty line have cell phones and cable television. In one of the most bizarre cases of misguided welfare in history, the American government is providing assistance for people to upgrade to receive a digital television signal.

If the majority wants to provide these social services and more, so be it. The payment for this generosity should be gratitude. Gratitude is the gateway to self-improvement. Entitlement breaks your will and can lead to social, financial and emotional instability.

Gratitude also nourishes humility. Through gratitude, you express appreciation for what you have, who you are, and where you are. You acknowledge the people and opportunities that have brought you to this point, and you recognize the talents and abilities you've developed during the process.

Gratitude is the key to authentic humility and Beginner's Mind.

The solution is for each of us to accept personal responsibility for our own success and happiness, express gratitude when we're the beneficiary of a helping-hand, and return abundance with generosity. Create material, emotional and spiritual wealth and then share it with others; after all, if you don't have enough, you don't have enough to share. Taking care of yourself is the first step toward taking care of others.

Increase your effectiveness, or power, and you become more valuable to yourself and others. You become a greater resource to, your family, friends, the people you work with, the people who depend on you, and the people you depend upon. You become more valuable to your community, your nation and the world.

A martial artist has a lot of people helping along the way. When I founded Northern Chi Martial Arts Center, I designed a crest to represent this. I found a clip art image that had three pillars with three small figures of martial artists, one on each pillar. The pillars stand for family, community and dojo; these are the three support systems that sustain a martial artist throughout his or her journey to Black Belt. The three figures stand for the evolving supportive relationships of teacher to student, student to student, and student to teacher.

A lot of people can help you along the way to Black Belt, but the work is still yours and yours alone. Support doesn't mean someone else sweats or bleeds for you; the blood and sweat must come from you.

Success is simple, not easy. All you need to produce this feeling of having enough is to maintain your motivation and discipline over the long haul. You've got to take care of yourself in body, mind and spirit and you've got to apply yourself with balance, focus and good timing. Do this and you become powerful; do this and you'll become successful.

This takes practice, not jealousy. Prejudice is the result when you start thinking the other guy is getting more than he deserves and you're getting less. As long as someone else is getting more than you think he deserves and you're getting less, you're looking at the world through a fogged over window. Clean the glass and take a good look at what's out there for you. Be thankful for what you have right now; whether it's a lot or a little, it is what you have to work with here and now. Wherever you're going from here, this is what you're going to use to get started.

Before we move along let's revisit what may have become the two filthiest words in the American lexicon:

Personal responsibility.

You're the only person responsible for creating your own success and happiness. As soon as you depend on someone else to drop success and happiness in your lap, you've surrendered control of your life. Give up personal responsibility and you've bought a lottery ticket. Of course, people do win the lottery, but why do most people who win big jackpots end up broke?

You can win the lottery without any talent, skill or ability. When you accept personal responsibility for success and happiness, you start the process of cultivating your talents and abilities.

Remember the key elements of success: you don't need money to be successful, but you do need to feel as if you have "enough" no matter how much or how little you have.

I'm always amazed by the wisdom of the American founders. For the first time in history they created a government that specifically declared that the power of the government came from the consent of the governed. Until then, governments were largely constituted to empower a monarch, usually with the acknowledgement of divine intervention. Until the United States Constitution was written, nations were institutions of subjects who depended on their rulers to assign rights and privileges. That's why people who were most willing to do favors for the rulers were the most privileged.

Along came a band of renegades who said no, that human kind was "endowed by their creator with certain unalienable rights..." The American government was not constituted to bestow rights to subjects; it was empowered by its citizens to protect and defend the rights of the individual. These rights were not given by the government; our founders acknowledged our natural rights. For the first time the government would be mandated to serve the people, not the other way around.

That's what freedom is all about. Of course, this privilege comes with a huge responsibility. If you want freedom, it's your personal responsibility to fully explore, exploit and express your naturally endowed freedoms of life, liberty and the pursuit of happiness.

We have the right to pursue happiness, not the right to happiness itself. It's your job to go out and pursue it. The best way to do this is to fully develop and express your talents and abilities, bring value to the world, and trade on that value as you see fit.

These are the only promises I ever make to my martial arts students:

> 1. Make it to Black Belt and you'll be able to do anything you want in life, within the scope of your individual talents and abilities.

> 2. You'll learn how to recognize and cultivate your talents and abilities.

Your most valuable assets never show up on a balance sheet: your talents and your abilities. Money can be lost or taken, fame and goodwill can fade away, and even knowledge can become obsolete. Your ability to engage in the process of developing your talents and abilities can never be taken away. They're portable. With courage and a positive attitude you can apply your talents and abilities to any number of new adventures.

Your talents and abilities make you powerful. We defined power as your ability or capacity to act or perform effectively. Power cannot be taken from you; you may surrender or abdicate power, but how can someone else take your capacity to act without your consent or submission?

Embrace the continual process of self-perfection; pursue excellence and you'll bring value to your life and the lives of others. Choose to be lazy or complacent and you may surrender your power and lose your right to pursue happiness. When you depend on others to provide your happiness, you're not just a servant or subject, you're a child.

Victory is not always measured in terms of survival!

Are you familiar with the Chinese symbol for "tai chi" or the grand ultimate principle of life? You might have called it, improperly, a "ying-yang." The two shapes that seem to be forever locked together in constant, interdependent motion are called yin and yang. One of the many useful meanings of this symbol is that life is a constant struggle between opposite forces.

The philosophy of tai chi recognizes that what can look like opposites are usually just two views of the very same thing; you might say it's a matter of perspective. You might do something with the best intentions, but you end up harming someone else; does this act make you good or evil? Do your intentions factor into whether this act is good or evil? An extreme example we often talk about in martial arts training, would be taking a life to defend your own.

You could make the argument that taking a life to defend yourself or someone else, is an act of courage and honor. If you're the guy who ends up dead, you may have another perspective; that outcome is obviously not desirable. The fact is that even when you're right, taking one's life is a regrettable act for most people. I've listened to cops and soldiers who have had to kill someone in the line of duty, and I can tell you from experience that good people who take a life, even when it's justified, come face to face with the horror of killing.

Every story has three sides; and we're usually pretty lucky if we can see two of them. You may be justified in taking a life to protect your own. The other guy may, from his perspective, have been justified in attacking you. The third side of the story is that it's usually a damn shame anyone had to get killed at all. Wouldn't it be nice if we always had the luxury of time and space to see the third side before we had to choose one of the others?

In real time in the real world, however, people die. You can apply that metaphorically to any aspect of life, particularly in business. Someone is going to win and that usually means someone else is going to lose.

That's why the Samurai would not always measure victory in terms of survival.

Success can only be enjoyed and fully experienced when you fight fairly and honorably. To the Samurai, it would be better to be killed honorably in battle than to survive if your survival was the result of a dishonorable or cowardly act.

Does this philosophy have any meaning in contemporary society? How successful were the crooks from Enron who raped and pillaged the retirements of thousands of people who entrusted them with their life savings? If the suicide rate of these rapists and pirates is any indication, I'd say their success was short lived and shallow. They may have enjoyed material success, but they were completely blind to the significance of emotional and spiritual success.

One of the most important ideas represented by the Black Belt is honor. It's too bad that honor is too often a lost commodity in our society. It's often a lost commodity in modern martial arts as well, but thankfully there are still plenty of sincere martial artists who are keeping this value alive. They provide a great example for how to succeed in life.

I don't want to scare you too badly! You don't usually have to sacrifice your life to express honor, but this concept of victory without survival can be very useful when you're trying to realize your vision of personal and professional success.

In my life and in my study of success and self-perfection, I've learned one, and only one, absolutely immutable rule:

Failure is an inevitable and unavoidable component of success.

What I mean is that successful people fail; and they often fail a lot! The old cliché says that the trick is to not repeat the same mistakes, but mistakes will be made along the way and there are always new mistakes to make. Sometimes failures aren't the result of mistakes; sometimes failure just happens. There are circumstances and conditions at times that are beyond your control; you've got to learn to keep moving even when things seem to be out of control.

Successful people persevere when others accept defeat; they stay focused on the discipline of self-perfection when others see only failure. That's a pretty good summary of Black Belt training! First you learn a new technique, or a kata. You might remember that a kata is a set of choreographed movements a martial artist uses to learn and practice fighting techniques. Kata is sometimes translated as "martial art dances." The literal translation of the word kata from Japanese is "form," but the more meaningful understanding to a martial artist is "correct movement;" you might call it an exercise in perfection.

Learning the kata is just the beginning. Talk to a lifelong martial artist and he'll probably tell you that a kata can never be fully perfected. Well, neither can real life; don't be discouraged. You learn the exercise and then you start to practice.

Once you learn a few moves from your kata, your instructor, or Sensei, starts the never-ending process of telling you what's wrong with it! "Bend your knees, deeper; back straight, eyes forward, keep your elbow in... straight line on that kick." Welcome to the dojo! You learn to enjoy this process or you leave. No matter how beautiful you make your kata, your instructor should be able to find something new to work on. The process is more important than the ultimate result; you might say the process is the ultimate result.

Year after year this process continues. You learn moves, your instructor corrects you, you go back to work and the whole thing starts again. After you earn your Black Belt, you continue to practice, analyze and perfect your basic movements; after all, isn't that what the complicated stuff is made of?

Is it the same in real life?

To achieve success you've got to develop a Black Belt attitude of learning, correction, and constant improvement. Living a successful life means embracing what Zorba the Greek called "the full catastrophe!" Failure and success are two parts of the same process of constant self-perfection. How you perceive your failures is what will determine ultimate success or failure.

The Samurai who died honorably in battle wasn't around to experience any sense of victory. In the course of normal life and business, you're much more likely to survive and I sincerely hope you do live long enough to fully experience the feelings associated with any particular success or failure. The fact is that everyone fails sometimes; and those with enough courage to live life to the fullest, will fail a lot. Those who can identify the external components of failure as a character flaw will most likely be able to persevere and eventually succeed.

In a moment of unusual boldness I once told one of my teachers that I'd figured out exactly how he had become a Master. We'd been reminiscing about all the students and instructors that had come and gone over his long career. His stories and his generosity in opening our bar tab led me to this great moment of enlightenment.

"OK," he challenged, "how?"

"You survived!"

He started laughing and admitted that this probably had a lot to do with it! In any vocation, the Masters are those who had the perseverance to stick with it while others died off or went on to other pursuits.

So…

Let's see if I can make some sense out of this painfully messy, yet beautiful process:

The first point I made in this chapter is that there are no guarantees of success; this is true. It's also true that success is yours at any time; you define your personal vision of success and happiness so you can declare yourself successful whenever and wherever you want.

Be grateful. Gratitude opens your mind and heart to abundance. You've got everything you need to create your vision of success and happiness. Open your eyes, ears, heart and mind and you'll see it. Any moment of life is a treasure beyond our capacity to measure; appreciate the gift.

Live the Rule of Respect; period.

Freedom is ultimately your decision to accept personal responsibility for your own success and happiness. The greatest responsibility you have is to continually improve yourself. Make yourself better and you bring more value to the world.

Share wisdom, love, and respect unconditionally. Share your valuable self with the world without any expectation of return. It's true that givers get; sometimes! It's more important to share your value with others because it's the right thing to do. Ironically, the greatest returns usually come when you least expect them. Sharing is the greatest expression of leadership; be a leader.

Embrace the process of self-perfection as your life's work; you'll never be without a job! Perfecting yourself is what Black Belt Mindset is all about. The goal, the work, and the reward is excellence…

…and you thought Black Belt was about punching and kicking?

Change the way you think about life, business & success...

...Jim Bouchard will turn your next event into Black Belt class!!!

Meetings-Conferences-Corporate Events

For booking information call 800-786-8502
or visit ThinkLikeaBlackBelt.org

Change the way you think about life, business & success forever. From now on...

...Think Like a BLACK BELT!™
ThinkLikeaBlackBelt.org
Jim Bouchard

Made in the USA
Charleston, SC
24 June 2011